T0339109

METAFICTION

Metafiction explores the great variety and effects of this popular genre and style, variously defined as a type of literature that philosophically questions itself, that repudiates the conventions of literary realism, that questions the relationship between fiction and reality, or that lies at the border between fiction and non-fiction. Yaël Schlick surveys a wide range of metafictional writings by diverse authors, with particular focus on the contemporary period.

This book asks not only what metafiction is but also what it can do, examining metafictional narratives' usefulness for exploring the role of art in society, its role in conceptualizing the figure of author and the reader of fiction, its investigation and playfulness with respect to language and linguistic conventions, and its troubling of the boundaries between fact and fiction in historiographic metafiction, autofiction, and autotheory.

Metafiction is an engaging and accessible introduction to a pervasive and influential form and concept in literary studies, and will be of use to all students of literary studies requiring a depth of knowledge in the subject.

Yaël Schlick is Professor of English at Queen's University in Ontario, Canada. Her research and teaching focus on travel writing, autobiography, American poetry, and contemporary fiction. She is the author of *Feminism and the Politics of Travel After the Enlightenment* (2012), co-editor of *Refiguring the Coquette* (2008), and translator of Victor Segalen's *Essay on Exoticism* (2002).

THE NEW CRITICAL IDIOM

SERIES EDITOR: JOHN DRAKAKIS, UNIVERSITY OF STIRLING

The New Critical Idiom is an invaluable series of introductory guides to today's critical terminology. Each book:

- provides a handy, explanatory guide to the use (and abuse) of the term;
- offers an original and distinctive overview by a leading literary and cultural critic;
- relates the term to the larger field of cultural representation.

With a strong emphasis on clarity, lively debate and the widest possible breadth of examples, *The New Critical Idiom* is an indispensable approach to key topics in literary studies.

Children's Literature
Carrie Hintz

Pastoral
Second edition
Terry Gifford

Fantasy
Lucie Armitt

Intertextuality
Third edition
Graham Allen

Literary Geography
Sheila Hones

Metafiction
Yaël Schlick

For more information about this series, please visit:
www.routledge.com/The-New-Critical-Idiom/book-series/SE0155

METAFICTION

Yaël Schlick

Routledge
Taylor & Francis Group

LONDON AND NEW YORK

Cover image: Best Content Production Group, Getty

First published 2023
by Routledge
4 Park Square, Milton Park, Abingdon, Oxon OX14 4RN

and by Routledge
605 Third Avenue, New York, NY 10158

Routledge is an imprint of the Taylor & Francis Group, an informa business

British Library Cataloguing-in-Publication Data
A catalogue record for this book is available from the British Library

ISBN: 978-1-032-01908-6 (hbk)
ISBN: 978-1-032-01907-9 (pbk)
ISBN: 978-1-003-18095-1 (ebk)

DOI: 10.4324/9781003180951

Typeset in Times New Roman
by Taylor & Francis Books

*Dedicated in loving memory to my mother,
Salomeia Schlick (1933–2020).*

CONTENTS

ACKNOWLEDGEMENTS

I have long been indebted to Ross Chambers, who first introduced me to the concept of self-reflexivity in narrative in undergraduate courses at the University of Michigan. His teaching and writings have been a source of inspiration for me ever since.

I was lucky to benefit from Shannon Minifie's astute reading suggestions, and from the insights of graduate students in my seminar on American women's short fiction.

At Routledge, I would like to thank Zoë Meyer, Chris Ratcliffe, Polly Dodson, Claire Bell, and Fiona Hudson Gabuya for their steadfast support in moving the book through its various stages. Particular thanks go to John Drakakis for his attentive editing and numerous suggestions for improving the manuscript, especially in terms of thinking through metafiction's relevance for earlier periods and texts.

In daily life and most of all, I am grateful for the unwavering encouragement of my family, especially my husband (and colleague), Glenn Willmott. His incisive comments on the manuscript and our many conversations about metafiction always led me back to that central question of why literature matters.

INTRODUCTION

An author boards a train, only to run into his own fictional protagonist: what shall I do with him, he wonders. For no reason that you can see, a story you are reading digresses to discuss the use of italics in fiction stories, and tells you that realism is an *illusion*. Part way through a different novel, page 132 suddenly introduces you to a new narrator who, like you, has read up to page 131 of the same narrative. A poem you are reading seems to address itself to you, chastising you for not paying attention and missing its point. The author of an autobiography begins to talk about herself as a female character.

All these are examples of metafiction. But metafictionality has been variously defined. It has been understood as a type of literature that demonstrates philosophical tendencies, literature that repudiates and questions the conventions of literary realism, literature that questions the relationship between fiction and reality, and literature that is located at the border between fiction and criticism or other discourses. Metafiction's resurgence in the contemporary period has been linked to poststructuralist theories that have, since the 1960s, increasingly reflected on the nature of narrative, representation, and meaning-making. It has also been linked to postmodernist

DOI: 10.4324/9781003180951-1

tendencies in contemporary writing that began with modernism. And it tends to be highly intertextual, aware of literary
tradition and its own place within it. While some theorists of
metafiction have seen it as a peculiarly postmodern phenomenon, others have stressed that metafiction is a transhistorical
element in fiction, dependent on the reader's interpretive per-
ceptions. The purpose of this chapter is to explore some of these
definitions and their contexts and to argue that metafiction is ultimately better understood by its effects than by its essence, by what it
does rather than by what it is. Subsequent chapters will therefore
explore what metafiction is and what it can do, examining metafictional narratives' usefulness for exploring the role of art in society
(Chapter 1), its role in conceptualizing the figure of author and the
figure of the reader of fiction (Chapter 2), its investigation and
playfulness with respect to language and the possibilities of fiction
(Chapter 3), its troubling of the boundaries between historical fact
and fiction in what is known as historiographic metafiction (Chapter 4), and, finally, its influence in the questioning of generic
boundaries seen in autofictional writing that, like historiographic
metafiction, questions distinctions between fiction and non-fiction
(Chapter 5). These chapters will address metafictionality in diverse
types of texts, including not only prose fiction, but also metapoetry,
metatheatre, and autofiction. Though certainly not all literature
is metafictional, metafictionality today is pervasive, even natural,
and the aim of the present volume will be to explore its variety
and permutations in the contemporary period.

DEFINING METAFICTION

Writing in the context of renewed experimentation in American
fiction in the 1960s, William Gass was the first to use the term
"metafiction" in his essay "Philosophy and the Form of Fiction"
(1970). In doing so, he hoped to align developments in the novel
and short story with similarly self-reflexive tendencies in other disciplines like philosophy, writing that "the novelist and the philosopher are companions in a common enterprise" (Gass, 1970: 5),
both are "obsessed with language, and make themselves up out of
concepts", both of them "create worlds" (Gass, 1970: 4). For Gass,

the "mature novel" is philosophical in nature (Gass, 1970: 26); it uses the medium of language not to render a world, but to make one from those already existing "forms of fiction" (Gass, 1970: 24–25). Just as there are "metatheorems in mathematics and logic, ethics has its linguistic oversoul, everywhere lingos to converse about lingos are being contrived," writes Gass, "the case is no different in the novel," where "forms of fiction serve as the material upon which further forms can be imposed" (Gass, 1970: 24–25).

In privileging the text's creation of, rather than rendering of, a world and in emphasizing its medium of language, Gass highlights what will be taken up in subsequent definitions of metafiction: namely, its repudiation of realism and its proximal relation to other discourses such as philosophy, with which it shares a medium and a practice. In signalling the metafictional turn of the novel as a culminating point of its development (its maturity), Gass also echoes John Barth's discussion of fiction's much-needed revitalization by means of self-reflection in "The Literature of Exhaustion" (1967). This essay contends that fiction has pushed through and rejuvenated itself through this new frontier; it has moved beyond its "used-upness" precisely by representing representation and thus, through such self-reflexiveness, has managed to renew itself. For both Gass and Barth much of this newness in fiction is indebted to the work of Jorge Luis Borges, whose *Labyrinths* was first published in English in 1962, with earlier stories appearing in translation throughout the 1950s. Borges, they argue, pushed fiction into the philosophical domain and emphasized its ability to reflect on itself. His story "Pierre Menard, Author of the *Quixote*" perfectly illustrates for Barth metafiction's power to create new forms from old ones.

In that story, we are told of the genius of one Pierre Menard. His "visible" work appears identical to Miguel de Cervantes's *Don Quixote*. But his "invisible" work is in fact richer, or so we are told by the narrator, purportedly a literary critic hoping to rectify Menard's reputation as an innovator and no mere copyist. It is Menard's "admirable intention ... to produce a few pages which would coincide—word for word and line for line—with those of Miguel de Cervantes" (Borges, 1964c: 39). While appearing identical, we are told, the meaning of their texts is not the same:

> It is a revelation to compare Menard's *Don Quixote* with Cervantes'. The latter, for example, wrote (part one, chapter nine):
>
>> ... truth, whose mother is history, rival of time, depository of deeds, witness of the past, exemplar and adviser to the present, and the future's counselor.
>
> Written in the seventeenth century, written by the "lay genius" Cervantes, this enumeration is a mere rhetorical praise of history. Menard, on the other hand, writes:
>
>> ... truth, whose mother is history, rival of time, depository of deeds, witness of the past, exemplar and adviser to the present, and the future's counselor.
>
> (Borges, 1964c: 43)

Menard's style is archaic in comparison with Cervantes's use of the current Spanish of his time; his reference in the twentieth century to "truth, whose mother is history" is "astounding" in not defining "history as an inquiry into reality but as its origin" (Borges, 1964c: 43). Menard's genius, Borges tells us in this mock story of literary interpretation, is to offer the new technique of the "deliberate anachronism and the erroneous attribution", a technique dependent on the "art of reading," not on the words of the text (Borges, 1964c: 44). The different meanings of these identical texts, in other words, are owed to its differing interpretation.

Borges's story is metafictional in Gass's terms to the extent that it does not "render the world" but makes one from the medium of language (Gass, 1970: 24); like Menard, Borges creates new forms from those already in existence (Gass, 1970: 25). For Barth, this story demonstrates how literature can renew itself, pull itself up by its own bootstraps by using existing fiction (Cervantes's) to create new fiction (Menard's, and also, of course, Borges's). Borges, writes Barth, admirably "confronts an intellectual dead end and employs it against itself to accomplish new human work" (qtd. in Currie, 1995: 166). Borges's metafiction also unsettles generic conventions in posing as a piece of literary criticism—is it a fictional story or an essay of literary criticism? It additionally unsettles interpretive ones in locating meaning in the reader rather than in the words of the text and in challenging the hierarchies of literary history that would have Menard relegated to invisibility as a mere imitator (or plagiarist) of Cervantes's work. A fiction, this short story explores questions of interpretation, history, meaning, and language, and problematizes the boundaries between fiction and reality, as well as between literature and criticism.

As writers about (but also of) fiction, William Gass and John Barth put these ideas about metafiction into practice in their own writing to reinvigorate a literature they felt had exhausted its possibilities. Barth's story sequence *Lost in the Funhouse*—itself in intertextual conversation with past canonical works by Homer, Laurence Sterne, Joyce, and others—depicts the life of his writer-protagonist Ambrose and begins with that most clichéd of openings: "Once upon a time." Except that here these words appear along the edge of the page, and the reader is given instructions about how to cut out the strip of two-dimensional paper, twist it once, and reattach it, thus combining the two phrases printed on either side of the same page: the first phrase is "once upon a time"; the second "there was a story that began" (Barth, 1988b: 1–2). Together they make up the "Frame-Tale" of Barth's short story sequence. This endless story now reads: "once upon a time there was a story that began once upon a time there was a story that began once upon a time there was a story that began once upon..." and so on. A Möbius strip, put together by the reader, this story is a never-ending beginning. Like Borges, Barth takes an existing and worn phrase as the point of departure for his innovation, transforms an old convention into something new, turns the reader into an active agent and co-creator of the story's making, and plunges this same reader into the dizzying and perhaps inextricable world of the text. We might periodize these writings by Gass and Barth as part of postmodern writing's beginnings, representing the continued process of renewing or extending the project of modernism. As such, metafiction might be fruitfully considered as a hinge between modernism and postmodernism, beginning the process of postmodernism's extensive use of self-consciousness, self-reflexivity, and intertextuality to pose questions about such issues as the nature of reality, the role of narrative and literary conventions, the construction of meaning, and the use of popular cultural forms.

METAFICTION AND LITERARY REALISM

In *Mimesis: The Representation of Reality in Western Literature*, Erich Auerbach charts the history of realism into the early twentieth century, examining each age's mode of seeing and representing reality. His final chapter focuses on modernism, "which dissolves reality into multiple and multivalent reflections of consciousness," responding as it does to "a Europe unsure of itself, overflowing with unsettled ideologies and ways of life, and pregnant with disaster" (Auerbach, 1953: 551). Metafiction is a later development of this same historical trajectory, one which, in particular, amplifies the challenges of representation. But even as historical discussions of metafiction address its pointed departure from literary realism and modernism alike, critics have also argued that it may be found across literary history. And, like the narrator of "Pierre Menard, Author of the *Quixote*", they have also explored metafictionality as a product of interpretation dependent on the activity of the reader rather than a quality inherent in a text, and as a mode of writing that engages intertextually with and is dependent upon other literary works. In her influential 1984 study of metafiction, Patricia Waugh makes clear that "metafiction is a tendency or function inherent in *all* novels," and is worth studying not simply because of its resurgence in contemporary writing, but also because "of the insights it offers into both the representational nature of all fiction and the literary history of the novel as genre" (Waugh, 1984: 5). Her own definition of metafiction paraphrases Robert Alter's definition in *Partial Magic: The Novel as a Self-Conscious Genre*, where he argues that "a self-conscious novel, briefly, is a novel that systematically flaunts its own condition of artifice and that by so doing probes into the problematic relationship between real-seeming artifice and reality" (Alter, 1975: x). Like Alter's, Waugh's definition seeks to distinguish properly metafictional works from ones that have metafictional tendencies by emphasizing that metafiction "is a term given to fictional writing which *self-consciously* and *system-atically* draws attention to its status as an artefact in order to pose questions about the relationship between fiction and reality" (Waugh, 1984: 2, my emphasis). Both Alter and Waugh emphasize metafiction's role in exploring the boundary between fiction and reality, and, in so doing, view metafiction as an important contestation of the conventions of literary realism. Metafiction's examination of its own "methods of construction," writes Waugh, also means that it explores "the possible fictionality of the world outside the literary fictional text" (Waugh, 1984: 2). Metafiction's very questioning of the boundary between the fictional and the real, that is, affects not only our understanding of literary texts and literary history, but extends to metaphysical questions about the nature of reality itself.

Waugh's detailed analysis of metafiction explores a variety of strategies used by metafictional texts—such as framing and frame-breaking, appropriations of popular genres, and parody—that disrupt realist discourse. Like Gass, Waugh addresses developments in other disciplinary fields, such as linguistics, philosophy, and sociology in order to show how pervasive questions about the nature of our reality and our role in constructing and mediating it have both led to and were expressed alongside tendencies among fiction writers to reflect on the nature of reality also; and, in doing so, to question realism as a style capable of representing the world as it is. Waugh's formulation of metafiction remains elastic and useful, allowing for a sliding scale of metafictional practices; it moves from works that explore fictionality as a theme, to those that display "formal and ontological insecurity" but ultimately recontextualize such uncertainties, and finally, to works that "reject realism more thoroughly" and whose fabrications "posit the world as a fabrication of competing semiotic systems which never correspond to material conditions" (Waugh, 1984: 19). Like Gass and Barth, she views metafiction's self-consciousness as testimony to the novel's mature state, its "recognition of its existence as *writing*" (Waugh, 1984: 19). Generally, she sees postmodern fiction as coterminous with the flowering of metafictional writing in the twentieth century, and views the most thoroughly metafictional works as mature to the extent of the thoroughness of their rejection of realism.

Recent metafictions as well as discussions of post-postmodernism have raised questions about the extent to which metafiction must necessarily reject literary realism. Indeed, Waugh makes clear the way in which metafictions of the 1960s and 1970s rely on realism to build their fictional worlds even as they trouble the readers' reliance on the stability of such worlds. In posing questions about knowledge and interpretation, metafiction can also be said to echo or represent very real philosophical and cultural concerns and so to mirror the historical conditions of the period in which they are written. The discussion of recent historiographic metafictions and works of autofiction in Chapters 4 and 5 of this volume will make clear how recent metafictional techniques draw importantly on and critique the realist tradition to make their point, and show how contemporary metafictional and postmodern writing today strives to newly engage with the material conditions of life. As Robert McLaughlin has argued, post-postmodern writers have retained the postmodern "fascination with representation, the layers of text, discourse, narrative, and image that construct our experience of the world" while aiming "to reconnect with something beyond representation, something extralinguistic, something real" (McLaughlin, 2012: 213). We can see this tendency in recent works like *Pym* by Mat Johnson or *Trust Exercise* by Susan Choi (discussed in Chapter 1), which take up pressing political questions pertaining to race and to gender all the while deploying postmodern metafictional devices.

METAFICTION AND CRITICAL DISCOURSE

Periodization in discussions of metafiction, despite acknowledged metafictional tendencies in *all* periods of literature, is useful to keep in mind as a way of discerning the development and intensification of metafictional approaches to fiction from the latter half of the twentieth century to the present. But important characterizations of metafiction have also emphasized its relationship to criticism and critical discourse rather than its reaction to earlier literary styles. Focus on metafiction as a kind of literature that integrates commentary about fiction into its own structure began right at the point that the term "metafiction" was coined. In his 1970 article on metafiction, Robert Scholes explores how metafiction "assimilates all the perspectives of criticism into the fictional process itself" (Scholes, 1970: 106). (We can see this tendency in Borges's story "Pierre Menard, Author of the *Quixote*.") And in her discussion of "narcissistic narrative," Linda Hutcheon defines metafiction as "fiction that includes within itself a commentary on its own narrative and / or linguistic identity" (Hutcheon, 1980: 1). She sees it as constituting "its own first critical commentary," and as a kind of writing in which "the distinction between literary and critical texts begins to fade" (Hutcheon, 1980: 6, 15). Such discussions of fiction's assimilation of and relationship to criticism form the central focus of Mark Currie's insightful examination of the philosophical underpinnings and historical trajectory of contemporary metafiction. He argues that metafiction is neither a kind of fiction nor does it have an essence. Rather, metafiction is a "borderline discourse" that can be understood as a composite of "inherent characteristics and critical interpretations" (Currie, 1995: 16). It is situated at the boundary between fiction and criticism (Currie, 1995: 2).

Currie's repositioning of metafiction and its definition is part of his exploration of the principle sources of linguistic self-consciousness in the self-referential emphasis of literary modernism and Saussurean linguistics (Currie, 1995: 6). He also examines how contemporary metafiction's dissolving of the boundaries between fiction and criticism echoes the way that poststructuralist writing traversed conventional boundaries between literary and critical / philosophical language. This can be seen in Jacques Derrida's work, where "literature's boundary with philosophy, linguistics and criticism is transgressed" (Currie, 1995: 8). Postmodernist metafictional writing, in other words, drew both on modernism and poststructuralism to create fictions that self-consciously commented on language and on diverse literary conventions within the fictional text itself. This definition of metafiction is agile enough to include works of diverse periods that rupture fictional illusion through explicit authorial interventions, or that dramatize the production and reception of art, or that are highly intertextual in nature. It also allows for metafictionality to be understood as the product of either literary self-consciousness or of critical renderings of self-reflexivity. His formulation acknowledges the way "any definition of metafiction is a contra-diction" precisely because metafiction's commitment to the idea of constructed meanings implies that it cannot be rooted in any essential quality of narrative (Currie, 1995: 15). This definitional approach is not only applicable to metafictional texts generally, but is particularly apt for describing the kind of metafictional writing that is called historiographic metafiction and autofiction. In con-tinuing to energize the meeting points of formerly separate or separable discourses and genres (fiction, history, autobiography), and in providing expansive meditations on the nature of repre-sentation itself, works of historiographic metafiction by such authors as Javier Cercas and Jonathan Safran Foer, and works of autofiction by such writers as Rachel Cusk and Carmen Maria Machado, might indeed be understood as metafictions. These late twentieth-century and early twenty-first-century works take such nascent generic troubling of the kind we see in Borges's mingling of fiction and literary criticism in "Pierre Menard, Author of the *Quixote*" and elaborate on it in order to make claims about a broad range of societal issues beyond the purely literary. They are border-line texts that insistently traverse boundaries and blend genres as a means of producing and provoking critical readings.

METAFICTION EXPANDED

In tandem with such evolving metafictional practices, writings about metafiction in recent decades have moved to accommodate expansions of the term metafiction, to move further away from thinking of metafiction as some essential quality that fiction pos-sesses, and to focus on its questioning of the boundaries between fiction and criticism, as well as between fiction and other genres of writing. Developments in narratology, in particular, have focused attention not on fiction alone but on narrative practices across genres and media, and have used metafiction as a model for thinking about the construction of reality more generally. David Herman's *Storytelling and the Sciences of the Mind* (2013), for example, explores how people make sense of stories and use them to make sense of their world. Metafiction's self-reflexivity, its attention both to the scaffolding of fictional worlds and to world-building, provides a particularly fruitful domain for such questions, and has allowed as well for descriptions of the experience of reading metafictional texts such as confusion, uncertainty, and the sense of a multidimensional reality.

We can see the usefulness of such cognitive approaches to metafiction for describing metafictionality's effects in both critical and metafictional works. In another of Borges's short stories called "The Garden of Forking Paths," a character by the name of Yu Tsun experiences a "swarming sensation" (*pululacion* in the Spanish, Borges, 1997: 117) as the various temporal levels of narration intermingle. Yu Tsun experiences this swarming sensation as he hears about a complex narrative composed by his own ancestor, Ts'ui Pên, from an English sinologist by the name of Stephen Albert. Ts'ui Pên had written a work whose subject is time and which is (like Borges's story) called *The Garden of Forking Paths*. This novel, Albert tells Yu Tsun, offers "an incomplete, but not false, image of the universe as Ts'ui Pên conceived it," representing "an infinite series of times, in a growing, dizzying net of divergent convergent and parallel times" (Borges, 1964b: 28). Yu Tsun, who is a spy, has come to Albert's house in the English countryside in a desperate attempt to signal the name of the city called Albert to his superiors in Berlin. He had no notion, prior to arriving at Albert's house, of the intriguing connections between this English sinologist and the work of his own Chinese ancestor. As he listens to Albert discussing Ts'ui Pên's masterpiece, Yu Tsun begins to sense all the possible universes that he and Albert inhabit: "It seemed to me that the humid garden that surrounded the house was infinitely saturated with invisible persons. Those persons were Albert and I, secret, busy and multiform in other dimensions of time" (Borges, 1964b: 28). The reader of this story, who is also reading about *The Garden of Forking Paths* in "The Garden of Forking Paths," feels their boundaries overrun and uncertain, the embedded narrative levels of the story no longer clearly discernable. This sensation of swarming is surely akin to Currie's description of the metafictional text's effects as the creation of "moments of critical vertigo in which the relations between real life and representation are no longer clear, either within or beyond the fiction" (Currie, 1995:

21), an effect achieved by the story's complex embedding of narratives within narratives and its troubling of fixed narrative time.

Recent explorations of the rhetorical figure of metalepsis, defined by John Pier as a "deliberate transgression between the world of the telling and the world of the told" (Pier, 2016a), have been important for discussing the relations between such different levels of narrative that are a central feature of metafiction (Barth's Möbius strip story is a good example of this phenomenon as is the narrative embedding in "The Garden of Forking Paths"), and theorists like Gérard Genette (in *Métalepses* 2004) and Marie-Laure Ryan (in "Metaleptic Machines" 2006) have elaborated typologies to explore the nature of the interactions between these different narrative levels and worlds. Ryan, for example, distinguishes between a brief intermingling of levels that is followed by the reassertion of boundaries between levels, which she calls rhetorical metalepsis, and ontological metalepsis, which "opens a passage between levels that results in their interpenetration, or mutual contamination" (Ryan, 2006: 207). These typologies build on notions of frame-creation and frame-breaking analysed by Erving Goffman in *Frame Analysis* (1972) and used by critics like Waugh to explore the alternation of the construction and destruction of illusion in metafictional works (Waugh, 1984: 29–34). They are helpful as a means of analysing and describing the intricacies of metafictional works and understanding their effects. Recent explorations of metalepsis also build on theorizations of narrative embedding in literary texts examined by such critics as Lucien Dällenbach in *The Mirror and the Text* (1989), Ross Chambers in *Story and Situation* (1984), and Brian McHale in *Postmodernist Fiction* (1987). The concept of metalepsis is useful not only for analysing literary works; it is also a means of articulating the structure and effects of diverse works in different media, and, as such, applicable beyond literary writing to a broader range of texts and representations.

The same applies to recent usage of terms like metanarration and metareference. While metafiction is fiction about fiction, metanarrative is, more broadly, narrative utterances about narrative (Birgit Neuman and Ansgar Nünning, 2012). Metanarrative is by no means a new term, but like metalepsis, was used by critics like Genette and Dällenbach for literary works predominantly. The term metareference (in lieu of metafiction, or self-referentiality, or self-reflexivity) can likewise be used more broadly, beyond the realm of literature, to discuss self-reference in all media or medial artifacts. In his discussion of the "metareferential turn," Werner Wolf explores interesting examples of metareference in such popular forms as film and children's books, such as *Shrek the Third* and David Weisner's *The Three Little Pigs* (Wolf, 2011: 9–15). Though literary critics and theorists are in a privileged position to explore contemporary meta-phenomena according to Wolf, there is still some reluctance on the part of scholars to "look across boundaries" and especially "medial boundaries" (Wolf, 2009: 4–5) to explore meta-phenomena. Though the present volume will focus primarily on literary narratives, it will also explore the instances and contexts that have expanded the parameters of metafiction, and, in addressing the question of what metafiction can *do*, will examine the functions of what Wolf has called "metaization" (Wolf, 2011: 4) as both a literary and cultural phenomenon.

CHAPTER OUTLINE

The five chapters of this volume explore different aspects of metafictional writing and different metafictional tendencies. While discussing some important classic metafictional works, they also examine more recent writing to discern new tendencies and developments in self-conscious narratives. Chapter 1 begins with a consideration of a variety of short stories and novels that blur the boundary between fiction and reality and between literature and criticism. It then examines the means by which such texts do so, focussing on narrative embedding, intertextuality, and paratextuality, and examining the workings of these metafictional strategies in three contemporary novels: Manuel Puig's *The Kiss of the Spider Woman*, Mat Johnson's *Pym*, and Susan Choi's *Trust Exercise*. These works demonstrate metafiction's power to produce valuable critique, to involve readers in questioning societal values, and to turn the space of the novel into a space co-extensive with our lived and readerly experience.

Chapter 2 turns its attention to the figures of the author and the reader as elaborated in metafictional texts and in literary theory alike to explore the production and reception of narratives. It explores the parallels between developments in literary theory and metafictional representations of authors and readers, both of which explore what Roland Barthes has characterized as "the death of the author," the reader's active role in creating the text, and the text's plurality of meaning. The metafictional texts considered in this chapter centrally represent the author and the reader (as in David Foenkinos's *The Mystery of Henry Pick*), address the reader directly (as in John Ashbery's "Paradoxes and Oxymorons"), and make explicit demands on the reader's experience and interpretive powers (as in Ali Smith's *How to Be Both*). In so doing these works explore the kinds of issues raised in reader-response criticism, in Roland Barthes's and Michel Foucault's considerations of the author figure, and, more recently, in postcritical considerations of the activities of reading and interpreting.

Chapter 3 turns to the material that makes up texts: language. It explores texts that are metafictional by dint of commenting on their own language and its ability to reference the real world (as in John Barth's "Ambrose His Mark" or in several stories by Lydia Davis), and texts that, through language games, highlight the artifice of linguistic and literary conventions (as in Lynn Hejinian's *My Life*, Walter Abish's *Alphabetical Africa*, and Christian Bök's *Eunoia*). These latter antimimetic or "unnatural" narratives foreground the text's artifice and extend literary forms and possibilities through creative linguistic play. Their "pre-elaborated and *voluntarily* imposed systems of artifice" demonstrate that "all literature is fundamentally combinatoric in character" (Motte 1986: 11; Motte 2009a: 723). The chapter concludes by examining Jacques Jouet's *Subway Poems* and Julio Cortázar and Carol Dunlop's *Autonauts of the Cosmoroute*, works that extend literary and linguistic play out into the experience of everyday life to explore its enriching potential. Such works extend Hejinian's desire to jam the ideology of language as a system through practices that resist societal structuration of urban life and travel experiences with the aim of finding new spaces of meaning.

Chapter 4 explores the crisis of representation that led to the questioning of notions of historical truth and to historiographic metafiction as a kind of historical novel that addresses such problems of reference in its very narrative. The chapter discusses the philosophical and cultural debates that brought about this new type of historical novel and details the salient features and strategies of historiographic metafiction. The chapter concludes with an analysis of two recent historiographic metafictions: Javier Cercas's *Soldiers of Salamis*, which takes the Spanish Civil War as its historical subject, and Jonathan Safran Foer's *Everything Is Illuminated*, a text that explores the way our relationship to the historical past is mediated by writing. The final Chapter 5, on autofiction and autotheory, similarly examines questions of reference and explores a new kind of autobiographical writing that questions the assumptions of classic autobiography and that, like historiographic metafiction, blurs the boundaries between fact and fiction to highlight the role of language and writing. Older autofictional texts like Roland Barthes's *Roland Barthes by Roland Barthes* are examined alongside recent works by Alison Bechdel, Rachel Cusk, Karl Ove Knausgaard, Carmen Maria Machado, and Deborah Levy to showcase diverse and new modes of self-writing as theorizations of subjectivity. In all these discussions, metafictional texts are understood as being themselves critical and theoretical commentary, as they insistently blur and question the boundary lines between fact and fiction, art and art criticism.

1

ART ABOUT ART
METAFICTIONAL NARRATIVE AND THE
ROLE OF ART IN SOCIETY

One of the important powers of fiction is its power to theorize the act
of storytelling in and through the act of storytelling.

(Ross Chambers, 1984, *Story and Situation*)

In *Story and Situation: Narrative Seduction and the Power of
Fiction*, Ross Chambers argues that texts themselves often
supply "the contextual situation that gives force, and point, to
[their] storytelling" (Chambers, 1984: 6), and that we must be
attentive to the text's own self-positioning, its self-referentiality,
as a means by which it tells us how it wants to be read. The texts
he examines are not explicitly metafictional or experimental; they
are realist or "readerly" stories, ones that typically lend themselves
to the reader's easy consumption of their narrative content. But
they all contain a complex, embedded narrative situation involving
a narrator and a listener. By interpreting these embedded narrative
situations and reading them as instances of the texts' self-reflection
on the nature of narratives and their power, Chambers explores the
force of fiction and the ability of narratives to transform human

DOI: 10.4324/9781003180951-2

relationships. His readings demonstrate the claim made in Patricia Waugh's study of metafiction, namely, that metafictionality is a tendency in *all* narratives—a tendency we can attune ourselves to in the process of reading and interpretation. In contrast to the realist narratives explored by Chambers, the metafictional works discussed in this chapter are ones that amply and explicitly situate themselves—and, by extension, fiction or art—so as to make their point.

This chapter will begin with a discussion of two tendencies in metafictional narratives derived from the various ways metafiction has been defined: their tendency to blur the distinction between fiction and reality, and their tendency to produce a critical discourse about various aspects of art and the artistic process. It will then examine the means by which metafictional texts situate themselves and make their point, and conclude with a discussion of recent metafictional narratives that work not only as a means of generating (literary) criticism, but as a means of reflecting on issues of gender and race, and, more broadly, on art's role in society: its value, its political relevance, and its power to mediate human relationships. We will see through these examples metafiction's ability, through its self-reflexiveness, to theorize about fiction and other art forms (as in Manuel Puig's *Kiss of the Spider Woman*); its ability to raise questions about sexism and racism (as in *Trust Exercise* and *Pym*, respectively); and its ability to discuss the political and social implications of past literary works.

If, as Chambers argued, the literary text's efforts to create within itself the situation that gives it meaning is, historically, the effect of a society in which literature is "an alienated discursive practice" (Chambers, 1984: 12), we might consider the metafictional text as working to overtly overturn its own sequestering: it moves beyond the literary in breaking down the clear boundaries between fiction and reality, it goes beyond literature towards adjacent discourses such as criticism and history, and it asks its reader to consider the very means of its own production as a literary artefact in the world. Also historically, we can see the rise of mid-twentieth-century metafiction as a tendency that implicitly challenges the period's so-called New Critical approaches and procedures for reading and interpretation, tendencies that conceived of the literary text predominantly as an isolated formal structure. And while some criticism of metafiction in the late twentieth century has considered it, in turn, as an exhausted form and characterized it as self-indulgent, solipsistic, or narcissistic—even calling its producers mere "crank turners" who produce "little pellets of metafiction" (Wallace, 1993: 142)—recent metafictional texts discussed in this chapter have been particularly effective in explicitly addressing the conditions of art's production and exploring the social and, especially, the political role of narratives.

Two sorts of tendencies might be discerned in such metafictional texts driven to self-reference. These derive from the definitions of metafiction discussed in the Introduction: on the one hand are those texts whose questioning of the relationship between fiction and reality works to trouble our sense of reality altogether; these texts usher in an ontological confusion about the nature of the real, or what is real, precisely because that boundary has been dissolved. In Waugh's words, such texts "pose questions about the relationship between fiction and reality ... not only [to] examine the fundamental structures of narrative fiction" but also to "explore the possible fictionality of the world outside the literary fictional text" (Waugh, 1984: 2). On the other hand, we have those metafictional texts whose self-referencing is put to work examining the structures of narrative fiction or art itself. These discuss fiction or art, address literary and artistic conventions, and situate themselves with respect to such broad discussions. This second type of metafictional text exemplifies metafictional tendencies highlighted by Currie and Scholes, ones that see metafiction primarily in terms of its dissolution of the boundary between fiction and criticism, as assimilating "all the perspectives of criticism into the fictional process itself" (Currie, 1995: 4; Scholes, 1970: 106). Such texts are explicit–maybe even aggressive—in producing the situation that gives them their point.

DISSOLVING THE FICTION / REALITY DIVIDE

Texts belonging to the first tendency often present the reader with two or more scenarios or contexts without indicating which serves as the ground situation or as reality, or that leave the reader to assume a scenario is real only to trouble that assumption at the story's end. The narrative strategy of such stories is to build two alternative storyworlds only to question them both, thus asking the reader to consider what is fictional and what is real after all. By the end of Julio Cortázar's "Axolotl," for example, we aren't sure if the narrator is a man watching an axolotl in the Jardin des Plantes in Paris, or an axolotl "who thinks like a man inside his rosy stone semblance" (Cortázar, 1967a: 9); similarly the reader of Cortázar's ingenious story "The Night Face Up" is left uncertain whether a man, who has just suffered from a motorcycle injury, is dreaming of the Aztec sacrificial practices during the ritual War of the Blossom while under anaesthesia in hospital, or whether an Aztec man being dragged towards the executioner-priest is dreaming that he is "going through the strange avenues of an astonishing city, with green and red lights that burned without fire or smoke, on an enormous metal insect that whirred away between his legs" (Cortázar, 1967c: 76). Borges's story "The Circular Ruins" and his "Dialog about a Dialog" operate similarly so as to disturb our assumptions about reality. "The Circular Ruins," like "The Night Face Up" uses dreaming as a means of both explaining the actions of the characters and of obscuring their ontological status. In this story a wizard begets a son through dreaming him into existence. He then wipes out the son's memory of his dream-begetting so that he "should never know he is a phantom" (Borges, 1964a: 49). His achievement of having introduced a dream creature into reality, a son, is complete, and he sends him forth to another temple. Travellers bring back stories of his son's miraculous abilities—he can walk through fire without getting burned. The wizard recalls that only fire can know his son is a phantom. So when a forest fire envelopes the wizard's own temple and he himself emerges from the flames unscathed, he realizes "with relief, with humiliation, with terror ... that he too was a mere appearance, dreamt by another" (Borges, 1964a: 50). "A Dialog about a Dialog" also questions basic ontological assumptions. In this short text, two friends (A and Z) discuss a conversation that A and his friend Macedonio Fernández had about immortality. A tells Z about this conversation at the end of which A and Macedonio Fernández had mused about killing themselves. Mockingly, Z says to A: "But I suspect that at the last moment you reconsidered"; to which A responds: "Quite frankly, I don't remember whether we committed suicide that night or not" (Borges, 1998: 295). These metafictional texts might be variously interpreted—as a parable about otherness in the case of "Axolotl" or as a critique of modern life, perhaps, in the case of "The Night Face Up," where hospital procedures seem not so different after all from Aztec rituals. Beyond their specificity, however, they all work by situating their reader in an uncertain zone between reality and fiction, waking and dreaming, life and death, making situatedness, in fact, impossible, and thereby getting us to question or re-evaluate our understanding of reality.

A more recent metafictional example of such ontological confusion is Charles Yu's novel *How to Live Safely in a Science Fictional World*, where the name of the protagonist, a time machine repairman, is identical to that of the author; where the future self of the protagonist of this narrative about time travel (chronodiegetics) has written a work that is "part engineering field manual and part autobiography" (Yu, 2010: 102) that is also titled *How to Live Safely in a Science Fictional World*; where we have included excerpts from that manual about Minor Universe 31 (MU31 for short) titled *How to Live Safely in a Science Fictional World*; and where this same protagonist is simultaneously reading and writing the book his future self has completed. Ostensibly this is a novel about MU31—a universe composed of 13 percent reality by surface area and 17 percent by volume, with the rest consisting of "a standard composite base SF substrate" (Yu, 2010: 28), an experimental test site for TimeWarner Time, a division of Google that operates various alternative universes for profit. But the reader of Yu's novel is gradually made aware of the text's farther-reaching critique of the chronogrammatical principles of this universe, where people live largely in the past, trapped in its time loops, rather than in the present. The antidote to this experience of "time as regret" is offered in Appendix A:

> Step out into the world of time and risk loss again. Move forward, into the empty plane. Find the book you wrote, and read it until the end but don't turn the last page yet, keep stalling, see how long you

can keep expanding the infinitely expandable moment. Enjoy the elastic present, which can accommodate as little or as much as you want to put in there. Stretch it out, live inside it.

(Yu, 2010: 233)

In this metafictional world, the book is that long-standing allegory for life, and reading for living. Both living and reading, it is suggested, can be active and inventive processes that forestall any predetermined future endpoint or narrative conclusion.

DISSOLVING THE FICTION / CRITICISM DIVIDE

John Barth's "Lost in the Funhouse" exemplifies the second metafictional tendency, to blur the distinction between fiction and criticism. It does so by interspersing its narration of Ambrose's trip to Ocean City with his family with all manner of disruptive comments about the nature of language, the conventions of literary realism, the typical structure of stories, and commentary on its own plot elements and characters. Often comical, it is also a serious consideration of the methods and role of storytelling—at once a story and a critical discussion of stories. As a metafiction it works to obscure the boundaries between its language and a critical metalanguage, between fiction and criticism. More recently Orhan Pamuk's *My Name Is Red* addresses questions pertaining to art more generally— its mimetic dimension, the contrary approaches of Eastern and Western art, and the politics inherent in its practice. This novel about miniaturist art is situated during the reign of Ottoman Sultan Murat II, and, more specifically during nine snowy winter days in 1591. It explores both the work and ideas of miniaturist art and artists, and challenges literary conventions as it does so: the reader's experience of having chapters told by different narrators—a corpse, a gold coin, a horse, or the colour red—is one means by which the novel explores the notion of perspective and point of view in art.

Rather than focus on narration or on art more generally, metafictional novels like *The Marriage Plot* by Jeffrey Eugenides address literary history and literary genres. The life stories of this work's three undergraduate protagonists are set against the heady days in American academia when French poststructuralism was beginning to take hold. Its central character, Madeleine, is writing a rather traditional final paper for a professor of the "old guard" about the marriage plot, arguing that the genre reached its greatest artistic expression with George Eliot's *Middlemarch* and Henry James's *Portrait of a Lady*. Simultaneous with her more traditional readings in English literature, she is taking a semiotics course focused on Continental theorists and is being introduced to the ideas of Roland Barthes and Jacques Derrida. It is a course where one prevailing idea, expressed by a fellow student named Thurston, is that "books aren't about 'real life.' Books are about other books" (Eugenides, 2011: 28). This is a sentiment with which the novel as a whole seems to agree: it is a book both about other books (novels as well as theory books) and at the same time a novel about the viability of the marriage plot itself. Its three protagonists struggle through amorous relationships and career aspirations to examine the extent to which this plot is viable in their own twenty-first-century lives, the novel here artfully fusing their life stories and its overarching metafictional exploration of plots more generally. Recapping its own plot and bookish concerns on the last page, Eugenides has one of the three main characters, Mitchell, ask Madeleine:

> "From the books you read for your thesis, and for your article—the Austen and the James and everything—was there any novel where the heroine gets married to the wrong guy and then realizes it, and then the other suitor shows up, some guy who's always been in love with her, and then *they* get together, but finally the second suitor realizes that the last thing the woman needs is to get married again, that she's got more important things to do with her life? And so finally the guy doesn't propose at all, even though he still loves her? Is there any book that ends like that?"
>
> "No," Madeleine said. "I don't think there's one like that."
>
> "But do you think that would be good? As an ending?"
>
> (Eugenides, 2011: 406)

The answer, and the novel's final word is, of course, "Yes" and the book we have just finished reading is precisely just the kind of book Mitchell has described: a book about the marriage plot that finally rejects the marriage plot. Just as Madeleine's love troubles began "at a time when the French theory she was reading deconstructed the very notion of love" (Eugenides, 2011: 19), so Eugenides's conundrum was how to write a book about the marriage plot in the wake of postmodernism and poststructuralist theory. Like Barth's suggestion in "The Literature of Exhaustion," he uses this old generic plot to create something new—a book called *The Marriage Plot* that explores the marriage plot's history, effects, and utility in the present moment.

HOW TO BE BOTH

The distinction between texts that confound the reality / fiction boundary and those that confound the fiction / criticism boundary is not absolute, of course. Most metafictional texts do both. *The French Lieutenant's Woman*, for example, veers towards literary criticism when it comments directly on nineteenth-century realism, disabusing its reader of literary realism's prevalent use of the omniscient narrator, who "tries to pretend" that "He" knows all (Fowles, 1969: 95); but the text also confuses our sense of reality when, after spending about a hundred or so pages entering into the lives of its main characters, the narrator tells us he has no idea who Sara is, that "[t]his story I am telling is all imagination. These characters I create never existed outside my own mind" (Fowles, 1969: 95). This is an instance of what Marie-Laure Ryan has called rhetorical metalepsis, one where extradiegetic and intradiegetic levels are briefly transgressed (Ryan, 2006: 206–207) or, what Monika Fludernik has named, following Gérard Genette, authorial metalepsis, because it is an instance of the author breeching the diegetic levels (Fludernik, 2003: 383–384). Such a manoeuvre momentarily undermines mimetic illusion and plunges the reader into uncertainty about where the boundary lies between what is in the fictional text (and thus fictional) and what is outside it (and thus real), or whether this boundary exists at all. That Fowles is interested in blurring the lines between what is outside and inside the text is all too evident later on in the novel when he, the author, tells us that he finds himself in the same train compartment as one of his main characters, Charles, looking at him and wondering,

"What the devil am I going to do with you?" (Fowles, 1969: 405). Metalepsis is literalized here, with the protagonist and the author co-existing in the same spatio-temporal plane.

Another example of a metafictional text where we can see the blending of critical commentary and a discussion about the nature of reality is Grace Paley's short story "A Conversation with My Father." The story seems to be about the writing of stories, with a father asking his storytelling daughter to "write a simple story just once more … the kind Maupassant wrote, or Chekhov, the kind you used to write. Just recognizable people and then write down what happened to them next" (Paley, 1994: 232). This plea for realism, with its clear narrative trajectory and nineteenth-century roots, is—much to the ailing, 86-year-old father's chagrin—a story his daughter cannot seem to write. Her two attempts at creating such a straightforward tale are peculiar, ironic, parodic, implausible, and unresolved. Their conversation about her different versions of the story also pits the father's traditional view of women (seen in their description, and their potential destinies) against his daughter's feminist approach to the art of fiction, her notion that the destiny of her unwed single mother protagonist is open-ended rather than tragic and foreclosed. Seeming initially to be about the art of story-telling, however, the story focuses by the end on a discussion of the underlying situation and context for this conversation—the father's impending death. For the daughter's storytelling divagations, filled with digressions and unrealistic plot twists that insist on one's ability to avoid a tragic end, is finally to be read as her desire to avoid endings altogether. When the daughter insists that her heroine could change, that her end is neither certain nor tragic, her father replies: "You don't want to recognize it. Tragedy! Plain tragedy! Historical tragedy! No hope. The end." To her continued remonstrations he replies with the story's last words: "'How long will it be?' he asked. 'Tragedy! You too. When will you look it in the face?'" (Paley 1994: 237). It is not, as in some of the examples discussed above, that we can no longer clearly demarcate the boundary between reality and fiction here; rather, the story shifts its ground. It does so subtly, not by the author introducing themself into the fictional action of the narrative as in *The French Lieutenant's Woman*, but by suggesting that the conversation in question is not really about storytelling, that it has to do with the situation of the telling, the story's "real" subject: the father's impending death and his daughter's reluctance to acknowledge it.

NARRATIONAL EMBEDDING, INTERTEXTUALITY, AND PARATEXTUALITY

Common to many metafictional texts is the use of narrational embedding, of intertextuality and of paratexts as means by which they explore and comment on a wide range of textual features, genres, character types, ideas, and their own narration as well. Embedding, intertextuality, and paratextuality are all also means of including multiple texts within the single fictional work, and this proliferation of texts and contexts—as shown in the various examples discussed above—works to proliferate the literary works' subjects and meanings also. Since the following discussion of metafictional works will focus on the embedding of fictional narratives within a fictional narrative (as in Susan Choi's *Trust Exercise*), on the use of intertexts and paratexts (as in *Pym*), and on the use of all three of these devices (as in *Kiss of the Spider Woman*), it is useful to define these narrative techniques first:

NARRATIONAL EMBEDDING

Narrational embedding is an instance where we have a narrative act within a narrative act. "A Conversation with My Father" is a good example. In Grace Paley's story, the father implores his daughter to tell an old-fashioned story, and this story contains two stories that she makes up in the hope of fulfilling her father's request. Such narrative embedding is always metafictional. It works to create different (and sometimes multiple) narrative levels or situations. Rather than transgress the boundary between real and fictional worlds (between what is extradiegetic and intradiegetic)—as we have seen in the authorial metalepsis of *The French Lieutenant's Woman*—narrative embedding reproduces these levels *within* the fiction. For, as Gérard Genette writes, "any event a narrative recounts is at a diegetic level immediately higher than the level at which the narrating act producing this narrative is placed" (Genette, 1980: 228). Narrational embedding means that we have a proliferation of authors, narrators, characters, plots, readers / listeners, and narrative situations, all within the bounds of the single, literary text. Most importantly, texts with narrative embedding typically feature discussion of those very texts that are embedded in the main narrative: in metafictional terms, the presence of embedded narrative works to turn the main narrative into a form of criticism. This is clear in Paley's story, where the embedded stories told by the daughter are discussed and critiqued in the conversation between father and daughter. But in creating a fictional world at the intradiegetic level, such narratives also lend a semblance of reality to the extradiegetic level, and, in doing so, blur our sense of what is real and what is fictional. In Paley's story the circumstances of the extradiegetic level are emphasized as real by the father's continued insistence that the daughter look reality "in the face," that she face the facts as opposed to creating fanciful stories that forestall tragedy.

A reader must also consider whether an embedded narrative is a model or, perhaps, an anti-model for the narrative as a whole, and what aspect(s) of the text the embedded narrative highlights, if any. In *The Mirror in the Text*, Lucien Dällenbach explores a particular type of embedding called *mise en abyme* that is characterized by its similarity with the work that contains it. *Mise en abyme* is a form of embedding whereby the element embedded constitutes a reflection or mirroring within the text. He details the phenomenon of the *mise en abyme* further by distinguishing this textual self-reflection in terms of whether the embedded narrative mirrors the *content* of the main narrative (as does the play-within-the-play in *Hamlet*), the *narrative act* (as in Borges's "The Garden of Forking Paths"), or the narrative's whole *code*. An example of a mirroring of the text's code—an instance of embedding that Dällenbach terms "metatextual"—is when, in Marcel Proust's *Remembrance of Things Past*'s second volume, we have a description of the artist Elstir's seascapes that constitutes a visual equivalent of the famous Madeleine episode. These paintings thereby "exemplify the author's own aesthetic theory" (Dällenbach, 1989: 98). But the elements mirrored by the *mise en abyme* can of course pertain to two or more of these: we can say that the play-within-the-play in

Hamlet mirrors both the content and the type of narrative act in question (the form of the play).

INTERTEXTUALITY

Intertextuality, which in a restricted sense is defined as the presence of one text within another (Genette, 1997: 2), is also a form of embedding. However, the text embedded into or referred to by the main text is in this case a previously published work, not an invented text. Examples of intertexts or intertextual references important to Eugenides's *The Marriage Plot* include Ludwig Bemelmans's *Madeline* books and Roland Barthes's *Fragments of a Lover's Discourse*. The first of these, the Madeline books, create interesting comparisons between Bemelman's heroine and Eugenides's protagonist of the same name; the second of these, Barthes's text, is introduced as a work Madeleine reads in her semiotics course. It serves subsequently as a means of structuring and commenting on Madeleine's burgeoning relationship with Leonard. Similarly, various novels that contain marriage plots—by Jane Austen, Henry James, George Eliot, and others—are discussed and quoted within the plot of *The Marriage Plot* itself. These intertexts work to emphasize some aspects of the plot, to draw parallels between Eugenides's characters and characters in other works, or to explore similarities and differences between Eugenides's novel and its predecessors. Like embedding, intertextuality usually implies metafictionality because the text is in essence both utilizing and commenting on other texts or particular aspects of other texts. While structuralist critics like Genette work to create typologies and terms to describe the complex relations between texts and intertexts, we must also note that intertextuality—articulated more expansively and philosophically by such critics as Roland Barthes and Julia Kristeva—is understood not only as a means of proliferating plots, characters, and narrative situations in texts, but also as a means of proliferating meaning itself. Intertextuality makes the text plural, dialogic, polyphonic. In "The Bounded Text," Kristeva emphasizes that any text is "constructed out of already existent discourse" (Allen, 2011: 35). Similarly, Barthes articulates the proliferation of meaning and the text's irreducible plurality in his discussion of the very word "text." A text is a weave of signifiers; it is "woven of quotations, references, echoes." The text's intertextuality for Barthes is not a matter of identifying or seeing some "origin of the text," some specific intertext that is at play, because the text is already linguistically and culturally plural (Barthes, 1986: 60). This broader definition is important to keep in mind even when exploring particular instances of intertextuality and their potential, local meanings, since embedded narratives, *mise en abyme*, and intertexts are all means by which literary texts underscore their inherent plurality and frustrate readerly attempts to reduce textual meaning.

PARATEXTUALITY

A final device used frequently in metafictional texts is the paratext. Paratexts are auxiliary texts that accompany or surround the text and so comment on its content or affect its reception. Particularly important to metafictional works are paratexts contained in the book itself—prefaces, editor's notes, footnotes primarily among them—and written by the author despite masquerading as external commentary. Paratexts create uncertainty about where the boundary of a text lies. As threshold phenomena, they are neither inside nor outside the text but in an "undefined zone" between the two (Genette, 1987: 2). Like embedding and intertextuality, the presence of such paratexts in the text are effective metafictional strategies for providing commentary on the text within the bounded text and for confounding the reader's sense of whether a text is real or fictional. In Charles Yu's *How to Live Safely in a Science Fictional Universe*, for example, one of the excerpts from the manual titled "How to Live Safely in a Science Fictional Universe" that the protagonist is writing provides a footnote at the bottom of the page. It tells us that the diegetic engineers Weinberg and Takayama mentioned in the manual are professors at the Center for Research in Advanced Narrative Dynamics and at the Imperial University of Lost Tokyo-1 (Yu, 2010: 155). But who precisely has written this footnote? Charles Yu, the real author of the text? the protagonist of Yu's novel? or the editor of Yu's book? The parodic content, of course, signals that these paratexts are indeed part of the fictional apparatus while mimicking the facticity of editorial notes. Many of Borges's fictions are far less discernably part of the fictional text, as many notes end with the words "Editor's note" in paratheses, as on the first page of "The Garden of Forking Paths" (Borges, 1964b: 19). In both instances, the detailed and factual nature of the content of editorial notes creates uncertainty about whether they are part of the text or not, about who their author is, and about whether the reader should understand them as fictional or non-fictional. In this way, paratexts are an important means of producing critical commentary about the text within the text, and of blurring the boundaries between fiction and reality. The discussions of *Trust Exercise, Pym* and *The Kiss of the Spider Woman* below will explore the subversive uses of embedding, intertextuality, and paratextuality in contemporary metafictional works.

TRUST EXERCISE: NARRATIVE EMBEDDING AND THE STORIES OF WOMEN

Susan Choi's recent novel, *Trust Exercise* (2019), is made up of three separate sections, all titled "Trust Exercise," each revealing a new perspective or new information about the section(s) preceding it, with all sections addressing the experiences of students circa 1982 in a high school for the performing arts. The first section, narrated by Sarah, powerfully conveys the atmosphere of the school, dominated by the charismatic and manipulative Mr Kingsley. He conducts trust exercises, thrusting his students into situations meant to undo their sense of themselves in order to reconstruct their ego in ways conducive to the art of theatrical performance. Acting, he tells them, is "responding with authentic emotion under made-up circumstances" (Choi, 2019: 27). But what is authentic and what is acted quickly gets blurred as we see the trope of acting or role playing used to describe events that are not strictly speaking theatrical: a budding romance between Sarah and David is described as David "finally stepping on stage in the role of her boyfriend. Sarah his girlfriend" (Choi, 2019: 17). When towards the end of the first section of the novel, one presented as written by Sarah, a group of English students accompanied by their teacher, Martin and Liam arrive at the school, Sarah and Karen end up in a foursome with the much older Martin and Liam. In the ensuing scene, Martin is described as having "cast [Karen] in the role of watching him, as he'd cast Liam in his multiple roles" (Choi, 2019: 105). When Liam forces himself on Sarah, telling her she is lovely, we are told he "delivered the line beautifully" (Choi 2019: 115). Though the line between what is real and what is acted becomes increasingly uncertain, it is nonetheless clear that the older adults—Mr Kingsley, Martin, Liam—have a kind of directorial power that the students do not possess.

Sarah's section also details the ways in which the line between teachers and students, between academic life and private life is also crossed by the likes of Mr Kingsley and Martin. Mr Kingsley seems to be having an affair with a star student performer by the name of Manuel. When his parents find out, through Sarah, that Manuel is Mr Kingsley's boyfriend, he disappears: "'Manuel's having family issues,' Mr Kingsley says smoothly. 'Hopefully he'll be back with us soon.' But he never is" (Choi 2019: 83). Joelle, too, mysteriously disappears. We only learn later—in the second section—that she is a friend of Sarah's, who, having become pregnant by Martin, has had to leave school in order to have her baby and give it up for adoption. Sarah's section conveys the intensity of these high school experiences, relating both the self-exploration and the testing of one's boundaries occurring in a place that is both enthralling and dangerous. Adolescents, they are experimenting with boundaries: what is reality vs. what is performance, being children vs. acting like adults, their life at school vs. their private lives. Sarah's section makes clear the enduring influence of this experience and of Mr Kingsley as a mentor, focusing on her own interactions with Mr Kingsley, her romance with David, and her encounter with Liam at a party. This first section reads like a realist novel. But even here, in the first section, so much focus is given to the uncertain nature of what is real and what is performance or to the lack of absolute knowledge of events (is the statement "you're a virgin" an objective or subjective statement? Has Mr Kingsley really been having an affair with Manuel or was Sarah just imagining it? Was Sarah's sexual encounter with Liam benign or not?) that the section teeters towards metafictionality.

Abruptly that narrative ends on p. 131. We learn in the book's second section that Karen, the narrator of this second "Trust Exercise," section has only read to page 131 of Sarah's novel and is now standing in a line of enthusiastic fiction readers to have her book signed by Sarah, her "old high school classmate, the author" (Choi 2019: 132). Actually she is not Karen: "'Karen' is not 'Karen's' name, but 'Karen' knew, when she read the name 'Karen,' that it was she who was meant" (Choi 2019: 132). Karen doesn't think much of fiction. She is not a reader of fiction. Sarah, she feels, has succeeded with her fictional work by "having aimed lower and chosen a talent anybody could fake with the right kind of tools" (Choi 2019: 137). Later Karen notes that the dictionary "tells us that fiction is literature in the form of prose that describes imaginary events and people, is invention or fabrication, as opposed to fact" (Choi 2019: 142). In this section, Karen takes Sarah's narrative to task for its inventions, alterations, and omissions. The facts Sarah has conveniently left out in her fiction, claims Karen, include the way Mr Kingsley abused his position of trust, Sarah's failure to understand just how vulnerable they were as children to his power, and what really happened to her, Karen, in high school. Sarah's fiction, says Karen, "left out the actual truth" (Choi 2019: 233). We not only learn from Karen that Sarah knows how Karen became pregnant by Martin, but that he abandoned her utterly after their brief fling. But Karen is not entirely despairing of fiction's ability to represent experience: she

> knows she's not a special kind of victim, for having gotten shown the ropes by a much older man who, it turned out, did not care about her. She knows this is perfectly common; just look at all the stories / plays / movies about it.
>
> (Choi 2019: 204–205)

Karen's section, in other words, critiques Sarah's representation of events, asserting the truth in response to her fictionalized account. In the process of correcting that vision, Karen's section not only fills in the missing information, it also poses questions about the past and about the nature of sexual assault. Karen is now working with David, her former schoolmate, on a play

Martin has written, and in their discussions, David talks about an article detailing sexual allegations against Martin. "We know they all consented," says David, then adds: "Well what about *you?* Whatever your thing was with him, you weren't some helpless victim" (Choi 2019: 193). But Karen's narrative—her objections to Sarah's story and her conversations about consent and victimhood with David—makes clear the long-lasting injury such sexual assault has on victims. And, in a denouement that has her take vengeance on Martin, she enacts her understanding of his guilt when Martin arrives to take part in the play's production, a play that itself, though in veiled terms, re-enacts a troubling scenario between an older man and a nameless "Girl." Karen wonders whether, for Martin, "there might have been no story at all." But his reactions tell her that "Martin's story, and hers, were the same" (Choi 2019: 190).

The third section, told by Claire, who turns out to be the daughter Karen had given up for adoption, returns yet again to the high school scene and also reconfigures the events told (by Sarah and then Karen) in the preceding sections. We learn that Mr Kingsley's real name is Robert Lord, and that, following his death, the school administration is planning to name the school in his honour when a "credible allegation of sexual abuse from a former student" leads administrators to reverse that decision (Choi 2019: 256). Claire, too, we learn, has met Robert Lord— initially at the school where she sought information about her birth mother; later at his apartment where, under the guise of providing her with further information, he lured her, then sexually assaulted her. Through the embedded narratives by Sarah, Karen, and Claire we see how the same story, the same experiences, can be variously told. Of them all, Sarah's stands out as the false, fictional narrative—the narrative that obscures where ethical / sexual responsibility lies and the power dynamics that underly various high school interactions between teachers and students. Sarah's skeptical attitude towards what presents as truth, revealed as fiction is thus understandably foregrounded in the second section. Yet, the reader must account for the fact that all three sections are named "Trust Exercise." All three involve the reader in a trust exercise with the author-narrator, raising questions of trust and truth, reality and performance, sexual assault and the nature of victimization. It may be tempting to agree with Karen that fiction is a talent one can fake with the right tools, or that fiction is opposed to fact, but even she opposes David's glib reference to Sarah's book as fiction, saying that the "whole thing about fiction not being the truth is a lie" (Choi 2019: 199). We may take this later position to be the point of Choi's fictional work. It is one that unsettles the notion of truth through its complex narrative embedding and its multiple narratives without closure. As Maggie Doherty has noted, recent metafictional novels like Choi's, written in the aftermath of the Weinstein revelations, "raise questions about the ethics and consequences of narrating such experiences—not just for the author, or for the victim, but for anyone implicated in story" (Doherty, 2020). Through narrative embedding, with narratives that criss-cross each other in time and trouble each other's certainties, Choi utilizes metafiction's power to probe the gender dynamics that engulf the stories of *Trust Exercise*'s characters in the wake of the #MeToo movement.

PYM: LITERARY CRITICISM, RACE, AND THE METAFICTIONAL NOVEL

Mat Johnson's *Pym* (2011) is a great example of how metafictional novels traverse the fiction-criticism divide in order to address questions of race and racism in American life and letters. Its engagement with criticism is made immediately apparent as the novel's protagonist is Chris Jaynes, an English professor, that is, a reader and writer of literary criticism. Hired to teach African-American literature, Chris, the only black male professor on campus, is denied tenure by his liberal arts college for refusing to serve on the university's "toothless" Diversity Committee. He has also steered away from his designated teaching of African-American literature to teach American literature in general, and Poe, his passion, in particular. The course he offers is called "Dancing with the Darkies: Whiteness in the Literary Mind," a course that explores "America's racial pathology," seeking in Poe and other early American works "the intellectual source of racial Whiteness" (Johnson, 2012: 8). Chris's course, "Dancing with Darkies," is a

direct reference Toni Morrison's *Playing in the Dark: Whiteness and the Literary Imagination*, a work of literary criticism
that centrally informs Mat Johnson's novel. Like Morrison,
Chris (and Johnson) is interested in Poe as a canonical writer
in whose texts we can see the workings of "American Africanism" (Morrison, 1992: 5): the use of blacks and blackness
as integral to the formation of white American identity. The
requirement that as a black American he serve on the diversity
committee and that he stick to teaching African-American literature is itself suggested as an instance of the unexamined
"racial pathology" that Morrison imputes to the American
psyche. Chris pleads to the college's president that his work is

> about finding the answer to why we have failed to truly become a post
> racial society. It's about finding the cure! A thousand Baldwin and
> Ellison essays can't do this, you have to go to the source, that's why I
> started focusing on Poe. If we can identify how the pathology of
> Whiteness was constructed, then we can learn how to dismantle it.

But the president's reply is: "Everyone has a role to play" (Johnson, 2012: 14). Chris, in other words, was not hired to question
racial categories, but, as Jennifer M. Wilks succinctly puts it "to
diversify the predominantly white campus by embodying blackness" (Wilks, 2016: 6).

Dismissed, Chris discovers an unpublished nineteenth-century
manuscript, *The True and Interesting Narrative of Dirk Peters.
Coloured Man. As Written by Himself. Springfield, Illinois 1837,*
that suggests that the events related in Edgar Allan Poe's *Narrative
of Arthur Gordon Pym of Nantucket* actually happened. Chris
embarks on a search to authenticate the differing accounts of the
two supposedly fictional, but apparently real, narrators. He also
hopes to find Tsalal, "the great undiscovered African Diasporan
homeland" described in Poe's *Narrative* (Johnson, 2012: 39). Here
the novel turns from its conceptual frame, one that blurs the distinction between fiction and criticism, to draw centrally on metafiction's typical blurring of the divide between fact and fiction. This
latter blurring lends the novel's zany antics and satirical thrust a
kind of truth status. Johnson's and Chris's roles part company here,

though not entirely. They both seek to investigate race: Johnson tackling the legacy of nineteenth-century American canonical texts (specifically Poe's), and Chris hoping to verify Dirk Peters's account, find the mysterious island—Tsalal—and redeem Peters by acknowledging this black (or so-claimed by Chris) man's discovery of a land "preserved from the predations of white supremacy, colonialism, slavery, genocide, and the whole ugly story of our world" (Johnson, 2012: 83). Chris's search for Tsalal—this mysterious land of blackness described in Poe's narrative—is made in the hopes of escaping "America's racial pathology." At the same time, Johnson's sustained intertextual references to Poe's narrative mean that literary criticism is never entirely displaced by the turn of events that makes the investigation of Poe's legacy real and literal rather than fictional and figurative.

Poe's 1838 novel details Pym's travels with his friend Augustus. They are first stowaways aboard a whaling ship. Then, after a mutiny, a storm, and an episode of cannibalism reduces the survivors to just Pym and a hybrid European-Native American by the name of Dirk Peters, they are rescued by a British schooner called the *Jane Guy* and head for the Southern Ocean's tropical island of Tsalal, an island inhabited by black "savages." In the novel's finale, only Pym and Peters survive the Tsalalians' ambush. They sail away with an islander named Nu-Nu, who dies soon thereafter. The nineteenth-century novel concludes with the men sailing away from Tsalal as they are confronted on the horizon with "a shrouded human figure, very far larger in its proportions than any dweller among men. And the hue of the skin of the figure was of the perfect whiteness of the snow" (Johnson, 2012: 229). This strange and racially suggestive ending has spawned a variety of responses. Morrison comments on the way "[t]he first white image seems related to the expiration and erasure of the serviceable and serving black figure, Nu-Nu" (Morrison, 1992: 32). In *Pym*, Johnson includes a discussion of various sequels to Poe's *Narrative* by Jules Verne and H. P. Lovecraft that respond to and rework Poe's final scene, and offers critical readings of Poe's "infamous final paragraph" (Johnson, 2012: 229–232).

Johnson's own tale of adventure continually references Poe's (and to a lesser extent Verne's and Lovecraft's) while exploring the complexity of blackness and whiteness and all manner of identities in between. For example, Chris himself tells us that he is a mulatto: "a black man who looks white" (Johnson, 2012: 135); his search for Dirk Peters's descendants yields one Mahalia Mathis, member of the Native American Ancestry Collective of Gary (or NAACG) in Indiana and leads to Chris's chastisement of "black American folks" who claim Native American ancestry (Johnson, 2012: 53). In this post-Poe tale of adventure, Chris and his buddy Garth join forces with the Creole Mining Company's crew and set south towards Antarctica to seek the remote island of Tsalal described in Poe's *Narrative*. The journey's destination is derailed when they are enslaved by a group of "prehistoric snow honkies" called the Tekelians, white giants clearly modelled after Poe's white shrouded figure but threatening (as the Tsalalians had been to the crew of the *Jane Guy*). They enslave the black crew, though Chris and Garth manage to escape to the Antarctic Bio-Dome erected and inhabited by Thomas Karvel (a parody of the American kitsch artist Thomas Kinkade). Karvel has built an artificial paradise in the Antarctic akin to the idealized land-scapes of his paintings. Chris and Garth, joined by the rest of the crew, survive the Tekelians' attack on the BioDome, which is itself destroyed in an explosion. Garth, Chris, and Pym, this last personage discovered (having kept himself alive by drinking an elixir of whale urine) among the Tekelians, finally set out for Tsalal with the help of Pym's instructions. He has already been there after all. The description of their approach to Tsalal inverts many aspects of Poe's narrative, such as the death of the white Pym rather than the black Nu-Nu, the appearance of giant black birds rather than white ones, and the sighting, on the shores of Tsalal, of "a collection of brown people" (Johnson, 2012: 322) rather than Poe's "white shrouded figure."

Besides its symbiotic relationship with Poe's narrative and with Morrison's discussion of "American Africanism," *Pym* makes use of various genres in its satiric exploration of race: the slave nar-rative or neo-slave narrative, fantastic and utopian narrative, and Antarctic tales of travel and exploration. The history of slavery and its aftermath are referenced when the crew of the *Creole* becomes enslaved to the Tekelians, who are caricatures of antebellum slaveholders. This enslavement is followed by a period during which Garth and Chris must work on their "plantation," like sharecroppers, in order to subsist in Karvel's BioDome (Johnson, 2012: 249). The two are allowed to live in "three-fifths of a house" (Johnson, 2012: 244), recalling the American Constitution's designation of a slave as equivalent to three-fifths of a person (Davis, 2017: 32). The BioDome itself is a figure of neo-conservative utopia. "I created this free land," says Karvel "[a]s blank as the morning snow. A clean canvas. A place with no violence and no disease, no poverty and no crime. No taxes or building codes. This is a place without history. A place without stain" (Johnson, 2012: 241). Like the notion of pristine whiteness that pervades the symbolism of many Antarctic travel narratives—its allure and history engagingly explored in such Antarctic travelogues as *Terra Incognita* (1999) by Sara Wheeler—Karvel's vision is antithetical to both Johnson's and Morrison's search for a historical understanding of race, in its desire for a paradise of ahistorical blankness.

Pym's exploration of racial ideas and fantasies and their formative roles in the construction of both national and personal identities in the text ends ambiguously, like Poe's text. At the end of the book, we do not find what Chris was hoping for: "the great undiscovered African Diasporan homeland...uncorrupted by Whiteness," a society "outside of time and history" (Johnson, 2012: 39). The "collection of brown people" on the shores of Tsalal discovered at the narrative's end is just as racially ambiguous as many of the racialized identities in *Pym* have been—those of Chris, of the Karvels, and the Little Debbie Treats-obsessed Garth, of those members of the NAACG, who, like Mahalia Mathis claim Native American ancestry despite what seems (to Chris) a group of people who look black. The aim of this metafictional novel's exploration of the roots of race and racism in the United States is finally to problematize the category of race and the idea of racial essentialism. It musters metafiction's capacity to write in the language of criticism and to trouble the divide between fact and fiction in order to critique racial systems and hierarchies, and to suggest corollaries to both historical and contemporary lived experience of Americans.

The text's argument is aided and furthered by its paratextual apparatus: its preface blurs the distinction between reality and fiction and its concluding "Discussion Questions" return us to a critical consideration of the text. Johnson's *Pym* opens with a preface where we learn that a Mr Johnson, "assistant professor of language and literature at Bard College, a historically white institution," encouraged Chris Jaynes to write of his adventure and to "present these revelations under the guise of fiction." Chris agrees with this strategy, for, "[i]n this age when reality is built on big lies, what better place for truth than fiction?" (Johnson, 2012: 4). The strategy duplicates Poe's, whose *Narrative of Arthur Gordon Pym* begins with a preface in which Pym details the advice of a certain "Mr. Poe" who tells him to recount his adventure and encourages him by saying that the "very uncouthness" of his book "would give it all the better chance of being received as truth" (Poe, 2010: 53). *Pym*'s concluding "Discussion Questions" mimic the kinds of questions publishing houses now frequently include at the back of the book to guide readers or reading group members in their consideration of the literary work. Obscuring the fictional / real and literary / critical boundaries, the questions included here ask the reader to consider the book's diverse racial depictions. The last question reads: "Discuss the end of the novel. Do you think that Garth and Chris have found Chris's paradise? If the story continues to mirror Johnson's version of Poe's narrative, what will happen when the figure on the beach meets both Garth and Chris?" (Johnson, 2012: 367). Like some of his other questions and like *Pym* as a whole, such queries steer the reader to explore the racial politics of these novels (Poe's and Johnson's) and use intertextuality to think through the literary and critical tradition and the need for rewriting American Africanism. *Pym*'s relationship to Poe's nineteenth-century narrative might be termed "parasitical" following David Cowart's schema of intertextual relations, because the guest (*Pym*) benefits from its reference to the host (*Narrative of Arthur Gordon Pym*); its reference to Toni Morrison's *Playing in the Dark* as "mutualist," because both guest and hosts benefit (Cowart, 1993: 4). Either way, Mat Johnson's novel succeeds in making its point in conversation with these and other authors, using the novel to create a web of intertextual relations that force us to consider the complex uses of race in American literary traditions, and are a means of addressing the very real sources and effects of fictional narratives.

KISS OF THE SPIDER WOMAN: METAFICTION AND THE POLITICS OF ART

Politics is similarly at the centre of Manuel Puig's *Kiss of the Spider Woman* (1976), set and published during Argentina's "Dirty War," a period of state-organized repression of dissidents, many of whom were tortured or killed. Puig's novel was banned in Argentina upon its publication. Most of its action takes place within the walls of a prison cell that is occupied by a Marxist revolutionary named Valentin and a gay window dresser convicted of corruption of minors named Molina. The many narratives embedded in the novel are Molina's retellings of his favourite movies. Some are made up by Puig, their retelling constituting embedded narratives. Some, however, are actual films from the 1940s and, though invariably altered in Molina's telling, are thereby intertexts: *Cat People* (1942), *The Enchanted Cottage* (1945), and *I Walked with a Zombie* (1943). These are popular narratives, traditional in their gender depiction and focused on romance. Molina retells these plots as a way of passing the time in their sordid cell and of escaping their harsh reality. They become the centre of many conversations between the prisoners about politics and sexuality, visual pleasure, and identification with filmic characters. Valentin and Molina's discussions about the implications of these representations work in the novel as a means of characterizing their opposing perspectives. Where Molina focuses on conventionally feminine details—the movies' depiction of hairstyles or clothing, for example—and on the love story, the revolutionary Valentin disrupts such cinematic pleasure by pointing out the repressive gender and class politics that underlie the movies' storylines. His astute commentary points out allegories, stereotypes, the psychic repression of some characters, and the movies' class biases, thus destroying the illusion and denying Molina the sort of narrative pleasure he derives from these classic Hollywood films. "Why break the illusion for me, and for yourself too? What kind of trick is that to pull?" (Puig, 1978: 17), says Molina after Valentin reduces Molina's depiction of the mother in *Cat People* as "marvelous," "respectable," and a "really good woman" to one who exploits her servants and is exploited in turn by her husband, "who forced her to do whatever he wanted, keeping her cooped up in a house like a slave, waiting for him" (Puig, 1978: 16).

The novel not only stages these moments of film criticism, but polarizes the reading / listening experience in doing so, asking questions about the politics of popular culture, and pitting cinematic and readerly pleasure against ethical and political concerns. The opposition between their stances is polarized further when Molina recounts a movie titled *Her Real Glory*, a piece of "Nazi junk" according to Valentin, but a "work of art" according to Molina (Puig, 1978: 56). Where Molina would like nothing better than to be subsumed by the escapist narratives of the movies, Valentin relegates their telling to night-time, reserving daytime for his scholarly reading in political philosophy. What unites their views and suggests Puig's point about the power of art is their common tendency to identify with characters and situations depicted in the movies. The movies serve as the novel's means of talking about the seductiveness of popular art forms and also work to thematize for the novel many of its central themes. For example, *Cat People*, with its recurring image of the caged panther, recalls the novel's own carceral situation; the depiction of the Nazis in the made-up movie *Her Real Glory* makes suggestive equivalences between Nazi Germany and Argentina under military dictatorship; and the invented movie about a race car driver, the son of well-to-do South American parents with revolutionary ideals, is an analogue for Valentin and for his own class guilt. So while the novel, through Valentin, continually questions the escapist values of popular artforms, it also acknowledges their usefulness and even their emotional validity. If we must resist narrative pleasure in instances of politically and sexually repressive representations, as this novel seems to suggest, we must also stay attuned to art's ability (as Molina says later of Bolero lyrics he sings) to "contain tremendous truths" (Puig, 1978: 139).

Such metafictional commentary on art and art's power is extended by the novel through its use of different types of discourses and their effects. Whereas the dialogue format is effective for staging Molina and Valentin's divergent views about popular art, the text's use of paratexts (in the form of scholarly footnotes that address issues of sexuality and sexual orientation) subtly re-enacts the oppositions we see on the character level and brings them prominently to bear on the reader's experience of the text as a whole. The reader is confronted with, on the one hand, the romantic plot of the main text (in which Valentin and Molina's growing appreciation and even love for each other is described) and, on the other hand, with the scholarly and drier content of the footnotes (some of which overtake the text, staging a battle not only for the reader's attention but for the space of the page as well). The footnotes differ both stylistically (in their tone and content) and visually (in their contrast to the main narrative on the page by their smaller font). While some footnotes hold local significance, explaining or commenting indirectly on the action of the main text, most comment more generally on issues pertaining to sexuality and gender applicable to the main characters. They are didactic and also (mostly) chronological in tracing developing ideas about sexuality, homosexuality, and liberation. Their succession—nine footnotes in total—provides the reader with a history of understanding of homosexual desire as shaped by repression and as capable ultimately of opposing patriarchal power relations. The footnotes tell a story all their own: starting with discredited theories and moving on to contemporary views about the liberatory potential of marginalized individuals. Given the protagonists' characterization, we might be tempted to align Molina with the popular art form of the Hollywood movies, and Valentin with the scholarly discourse of the footnotes. The mutual understanding and love that develops between the prisoners leads us to consider the way that, just like Valentin comes together with Molina in an unlikely love, so the novel's juxtaposition of "seductive storytelling and oppressive scholarly prose" can create an unlikely union in this text, one that works to mediate between these opposing textual spaces (Chambers, 1991: 229). The point is we need both: both head and heart, both the rational scholarly discourse of the footnotes and a discourse of the heart. The paratexts also function to re-enact the dynamic between centre (main text) and margin (the footnotes, as well as the prisoners, whose differently marginalized positions are made clear from the outset). Like the embedded narratives in this novel, its paratextual matter simultaneously gestures at oppositions that are ethical and political in nature *and* suggests that they must be resolved if gender or class liberation and equality are to be realized.

The novel's metafictional apparatus is furthered by its inclusion of yet additional types of discourses: not only the form of the dialogue and of footnotes, but also the distanced third person narration we encounter in chapters represented as reports on the two prisoners by prison officials. These reports are clinical, factual, and detailed renditions of the lives of the prisoners from another perspective. They allow us to see how the carceral system sees the protagonists–as carceral subjects who are marginal and devalued. These reports show us the characters in a different light and with neither compassion nor understanding: "11:04 a.m. subject received phone call from relatives" (Puig, 1978: 265) or

> the possibilities of a hidden code based upon the various feminine names employed by the subject in addressing the above-mentioned Lalo, it should be stressed that the tone of the conversations was continually bantering and the conversations themselves extremely disordered. Nonetheless, the matter will be watched further.
>
> (Puig, 1978: 266)

It is through such a report—"typed up in quadruplicate, for distribution only to authorized personnel, with the original to remain in this office permanently on file" (Puig, 1978: 274) —that we learn of Molina's death in a shootout between the military police and "the extremists," allies of Valentin. These reports, as Ross Chambers has argued, not only show us the objectification of Valentin and Molina, they also "transform the metaphor of reading as movie viewing into the metaphor of reading as social surveillance" (Chambers, 1991: 230). The novel works, that is, both by seducing the reader and drawing them into the surprisingly rich emotional and intellectual lives of the prisoners, and by showing the reader the ways in which they are part of the prison and its system of surveillance, implicated in broad systems of oppression.

All three novels discussed above use the metafictional devices of embedded narratives, intertextuality, and paratextuality to address issues of gender, race, art, and representation within specific historical and national contexts: the emergence of the #MeToo movement in *Trust Exercise*, the re-evaluation of racial relations in contemporary America and its literary canon in *Pym*, and the critique of military dictatorship in Argentina in *Kiss of the Spider Woman*. As Mary Holland has stressed in her recent discussion of postmodern metafiction, such texts do not compromise readerly immersion or engage in empty post-modern antics, but address the powerful and transformative potential of reading and re-reading (Holland, 2013: 190–193). Their complex narratives and narrative structures—always in dialogue with other modes of representation and diverse points of view—reveal metafiction's capacity for producing powerful critiques by theorizing about fiction and fictionality, and by examining storytelling through the act of storytelling.

2

RETHINKING THE AUTHOR AND ACTIVATING THE READER IN METAFICTION

The previous chapter focused on metafictional narratives, paying special attention to their use of narrative embedding and intertextuality and to their use of paratexts as means of obscuring the dividing lines between fiction and reality and of producing self-reflexive commentaries on narrative itself. This chapter will focus on metafiction's use of two figures essential to fiction: the figure of the author and the figure of the reader. We may think of these entities as forms of figural rather than narrational embedding (Chambers, 1984: 33), and, when they are prominent in metafictional texts, as a means by which texts comment on the production and reception of narrative. It is no coincidence that the figure of the author and the figure of the reader assumed particular importance in contemporary metafictional works at the same time that they also gained in importance in critical and theoretical discussions about literature and interpretation. Indeed, the rise of contemporary metafiction through the 1960s and 1970s was coterminous with

DOI: 10.4324/9781003180951-3

the heyday of reader-response criticism that sought to examine issues of reception. Metafiction's preoccupation with the figures of the author and the reader also occurred at the same time that theoretical debates about the ideological and interpretive implications of the concept of the author were being written about by Roland Barthes and Michel Foucault, a period during which the "text" and its plurality of meaning was increasingly replacing notions of the author, the author's "work," and the author's intention.

This chapter will begin by considering some depictions of the author in metafiction. These are depictions that both scrutinize the figure of the author and question their authority—in both moral terms and in terms of their ability to control textual meaning. It will then turn to examine the figures of the author and the reader in reader-response criticism, and in the writings of Roland Barthes and Michel Foucault to show how metafictional discussions parallel those occurring in critical and theoretical discourse. Barthes is a key figure in theorizing and reorienting contemporary understanding of the author and the reader, and his self-conscious critical writing underscores reading as the creative process through which the text is realized. In exploring reading as a creative process, Barthes interestingly problematizes the same boundary between criticism and creative writing that metafiction does, and foregrounds the reader as an active producer of the text in ways that metafiction does also. This chapter will conclude with a consideration of recent discussions of the readerly experience in the field of cognitive narratology, and with an examination of recent metafictional texts that highlight the importance of the active role of the reader and strive to theorize the complex relationship between the author and the reader within the fictional text itself. This chapter's alternation between its analysis of metafiction and criticism / theory suggests not only the dialectic relationship between these discourses, but the ways in which metafiction can be read *as* literary theory.

REPRESENTING THE AUTHOR IN METAFICTION

It is tempting to see metafiction as spearheading this trend to reconsider the roles of author and reader if we look again at the work of J. L. Borges and his short story "Pierre Menard, Author of the *Quixote*" that was discussed in the Introduction. Originally published in 1939, it addresses many of the issues that reader-response criticism and theoretical discussions about the author and the reader later developed. It focuses on the following: (i) the extent to which the author controls the text's meaning or functions as a key figure for literary interpretation; (ii) whether different responses to literary works produce identical or similar meanings; (iii) the degree to which the text can sustain as many meanings as readers wish to create, and (iv) whether some readers' interpretations are more valid than others. Pierre Menard is a reader-author, one who has reproduced exactly the words of an older, canonical author. In so doing, the story claims, he "has enriched ... the halting and rudimentary art of reading" (Borges, 1964c: 44). We see this focus on the power of reading to produce meanings beyond the author's original text expressed also by circumspect treatments of the authority of the author figure in Fowles's *The French Lieutenant's Woman*, discussed in Chapter 1. Here, the novel's author figure disabuses its reader of the notion of an omniscient narrator and of clinging to the idea of a novelist who controls his characters: "a genuinely created world," we are told in chapter 13 of the novel, "must be independent of its creator" (Fowles, 1969: 96). This novel's plural endings further force its reader to negotiate the text's multiple, potential outcomes. In the first of these endings, Charles returns to Ernestina, his betrothed. The order of the following two additional endings is, we are told, decided by the author's flip of a coin (Fowles, 1969: 406) with the result that the first of these consists of Charles finding Sarah, rekindling his love for her, and recognizing his daughter Lalage; and the second consists of Charles finding Sarah, but, due to a series of misunderstandings, storming out of her house without recognizing his own daughter Lalage. The arbitrary order of the final two endings and the author figure's explicit relinquishing of control over narrative order means that the reader must make up their own mind about the novel's conclusion and meaning.

In more recent metafictions, too, there is a tendency to view the author with some suspicion and to critique this figure. In Julian Barnes's *Flaubert's Parrot*, the quest to find the "real" parrot Flaubert used in his realist short story "*Un Coeur Simple*" is part of a cult of the author, a desire to get at some truth pertaining to Flaubert's creative process. But the quest yields no definitive conclusions, as various museums offer different parrots all claiming to be the model Flaubert used. Upon first seeing one of these parrots, the narrator feels "moved and cheered," feeling he "had almost known the writer" (Barnes, 2009: 16). But the novel's conclusion questions this narrator's author-obsession; emblematically, he is forced to confront the demise of the cult of the author signalled by the various statues of Gustave Flaubert, all in a state of disrepair. In this passage from the penultimate page of the novel, the narrator says farewell to the author, and, in likening himself to a doctor, pays final and dubious tribute to the author's ailing figure(s):

> It was time to pay farewell. Like a conscientious doctor, I made the round of Flaubert's three statues. What shape was he in? At Trouville his moustache still needs repair; though the patching on his thigh now looks less conspicuous. At Barentin, his left leg is beginning to split, there is a hole in the corner of his jacket, and a mossy discoloration spots his upper body; I stared at the greenish marks on his chest, half-closed my eyes, and tried to turn him into a Carthaginian interpreter. At Rouen, in the place des Carmes, he is structurally sound, confident in his alloy of 93 per cent copper and 7 per cent tin; but he still continues to streak. Each year he seems to cry a couple more cupreous tears, which brightly vein his neck.
>
> (Barnes, 2009: 189)

Like the parrots, this author figure is no singular entity. And, besides his now multiple existences or meanings, the statues insist that the cult of the author is, like realism, according to this novel, a thing of the past.

In Ian McEwan's *Atonement*, the author figure is also scrutinized. Briony Tallis is a fantasist, whose storytelling misconstrues reality, and brings about disastrous consequences for several of the novel's characters. In the final section of the book, titled "London 1999," we encounter Briony, who is now a successful writer. But, like Flaubert's ailing statues, her diagnosis of vascular dementia signals her decline and approaching death quite beyond the harmful consequences of her storytelling. A similar critique of the author can be seen in Susan Choi's *Trust Exercise*, discussed in Chapter 1. In part two of the novel, we meet Karen, who frequently refers to Sarah, the author of the first part of the novel, as "[h]er old high school classmate, the author." Sarah is an author figure who has manipulated the facts to her own advantage. After discussing her own, different career trajectory in dance, Karen concludes that Sarah—the author—"struck much the same pose, but with writing. Scribble, scribble, scribble went Sad Sarah in her Solemn Notebook. The only difference being that Sarah succeeded, having aimed lower and chosen a talent anybody could fake with the right kind of tools" (Choi, 2019: 136–137). While we may not take this charge against the author entirely seriously, it is altogether clear that Choi pushes her reader to reconsider the authority of the writer.

In David Foenkinos's recent satire of the celebrity-author and the publishing industry, we see a different dimension of authorship scrutinized. *The Mystery of Henri Pick* is metafictional not only because it insistently foregrounds the production and reception of fiction, but also because it plays intertextual games with Richard Brautigan's 1971 love story, *The Abortion: An Historical Romance 1966*. In *The Abortion*, Brautigan's invented male librarian decides to set up a library of works rejected by publishers, a fictional idea that was later realized by an actual library in Vancouver, Washington dubbed The Brautigan Library (see its website: thebrautiganlibrary.org). Foekinos seizes on Brautigan's idea, returning it to the domain of fiction and locating it in Crozon, France, where Foenkinos's reclusive librarian, Jean-Pierre Gourvec, has set up just such a rejected manuscript library collection. It is from this library that a rising star of the Parisian publisher Grasset and an avid book lover by the name of Delphine Despero claims to have found the surprising masterpiece titled *The Last Hours of a Love Affair* by one Henri Pick, a deceased Breton Pizzeria owner. It is a novel about the final moments of a love affair made unique because descriptions of Pushkin's death parallel the romantic plot. Sensing that the story of this found manuscript will itself create an interest in the novel, Delphine deftly managed the publication of Pick's novel, publicizing the book but saying as little as possible about it. The novel becomes a sensation: Henri Pick's widow and daughter are hounded by journalists wanting to find out more about the mysterious author who produced such a work. Henri's wife and daughter are initially dubious that Henri could have written this book, since he never so much as wrote a Valentine's Day card or even bothered to write the day's specials on the chalkboard outside the restaurant (Foenkinos, 2020: 74). But little by little the wife "gave herself entirely to this new reality." Perhaps her husband had been inspired by the early days of their love affair, she thinks. Gradually her idea of her deceased husband begins to change (Foenkinos, 2020: 78). Joséphine, Henri's daughter, is also initially incredulous, but then starts thinking of her father differently: "Now she thought that all his silences, the way he gradually erased himself from the world, had perhaps been a way of hiding his poetic soul" (Foenkinos, 2020: 96).

In this exploration of the cult of the author, the author's mystique and the story behind the novel's discovery are what matter and what the publishing industry capitalizes on with surprising and spectacular results. The romantic idea of an author not seeking publication, of the lone, creative soul dedicating himself to writing after long hours of work at the pizzeria, of being finally discovered and celebrated after death takes immediate hold. The consequences of Henri Pick's meteoric rise are multiple and profound: several love affairs begin and several end as a result of the publication and success of the novel; the book becomes the number one bestseller in France; a new trend in publishing rejected manuscripts takes hold; Pick is compared to J. D. Salinger and to Thomas Pynchon; sales in Henri Pick's daughter's lingerie shop get a boost; fans begins to flock to Crozon to visit Henri Pick's gravesite; "[e]ven sales of Pushkin went up" (Foenkinos, 2020: 125). In the end, a journalist reveals that the real author is Gourvec, the librarian who had several of his own manuscripts rejected and who consequently set up the library of rejected manuscripts.

But in fact, the author is the literary agent's partner, Frédéric Koskas. Delphine had fallen in love with him after reading his first novel *The Bathtub*, a novel she enthusiastically promoted at Grasset but one that had little success upon publication. Together they had plotted to present Koskas's next novel (titled *The Bed*) as a manuscript by Pick that they found in the rejected books library, hoping to reveal the true identity of the author later.

Resentful of *The Bathtub*'s failure as opposed to the success of his second novel (retitled and masquerading as Pick's), Koskas embarks on yet another novel titled *The Man Who Told the Truth* that exposes the details of the Henri Pick affair but also provides "a philosophical analysis of our current society's focus on form over substance" (Foenkinos, 2020: 279). In the end, Delphine and Frédéric decide it is best to leave things as they are, and *The Man Who Told the Truth* is duly deposited in the library of rejected books. This madcap mystery about the figure of the author and the publishing industry that sustains him is of course just such an analysis of "society's obsession with form over substance." That two books by the same author have such differing receptions is not due to anything *in* the texts, but to the social and cultural phenomenon surrounding the unusual circumstances of the second book's publication and promotion. The far-reaching economic, romantic, and literary consequences of the cult of the author in Pick's case, suggests Foenkinos, are quite real.

LITERARY THEORY AND THE DEATH OF THE AUTHOR

Not all literary representations of the author are negative, of course. But such modern scrutiny of the figure of the author echoes the critiques levelled at the author figure in literary theory since the late 1960s and early 1970s. Both Roland Barthes and Michel Foucault see the author function as an historical and ideological construct that impedes and limits the free circulation of the text's meaning. The author is "a certain functional principle," writes Foucault, "by which, in our culture, one limits, excludes, and chooses; in short, by which one impedes the free circulation, the free manipulation, the free composition, decomposition, and recomposition of fiction" (Foucault, 1984: 119). Barthes similarly associates the author with such economic and conservative values, writing that the author is "the father and the owner of his work" (Barthes, 1977b: 160). To abide by the value of the author means that we strive to decipher a work: in other words, that we read to find the author's meaning. In a thorough-going critique, Barthes contrasts the values of the author and his Work with the idea of the Text. Unlike the Work, the Text's meaning is plural, irreducible; and whereas the Work is the object of

the reader's consumption, the Text is the object of the reader's production. The call for the death of the author signals that they no
longer control the text's meaning. This death is linked directly by
Barthes to the birth of the reader. He acknowledges, of course, the
presence of the author in culture and frequently refers to authors
like Balzac, Mallarmé, and Proust in his writings. But in favouring
the notion of the Text and its plurality, he questions the author's
dominance and control over the meaning of the text: "It is not that
the Author may not 'come back' in the Text, in his text," he writes,
"but he then does so as a 'guest' … no longer privileged, paternal,
aletheological" (Barthes, 1977b: 161). While Barthes's position
echoes W. K. Wimsatt and Monroe Beardsley's formulation of the
"Intentional Fallacy," which argues that the author's intention is
"neither available nor desirable" (Wimsatt and Beardsley, 1946:
468), Barthes importantly neither excludes *nor* privileges authorial
intention. In radically opening up the Text to signification, he aims
emphatically to avoid delimiting its potential meanings.

While Barthes's aim in the essays "The Death of the Author" and
"From Work to Text" is to critique the author and to assert instead
the role of the reader, other of his works strive to *enact* precisely the
kind of liberatory reading practices that the notion of the Text was
meant to facilitate. Though he maintains a distinction between the
consumption of the Work and the production of the Text ("From
Work to Text"), between the "readerly" nature of the Work and the
"writerly" nature of the Text (*S / Z*), and between the classical or
realist text's production of pleasure as opposed to the modernist
text's production of bliss (*The Pleasure of the Text*), his own writing
increasingly models the kind of creative reading that turns even
classical, realist texts into writerly ones, produced rather than consumed by the reader. This is the intention of *S / Z*, a book in which
Barthes takes a short story by Balzac and illustrates the plurality of
this supposedly consumable, readerly, classical, realist text, showing
"the stereographic plurality of its weave of signifiers" (Barthes,
1977b: 159). This kind of writing interestingly does something that
resembles what metafictional works do too, and that Barthes noted
in his essay "Literature and Metalanguage": it blurs the lines
between creative and interpretive language, between literature and
commentary on literature, between writing and reading. It does so,

importantly, and as Barthes suggests with respect to literary criticism, in a way that is directed toward "a construction of the intelligibility of our own time" (Barthes, 1972a: 260). This is precisely the quality possessed by Pierre Menard's *Don Quixote* in relation to that very same text by Cervantes. Like Borges, Barthes, too, insists that reading—that is, the process of producing the text—can fill even "the most placid works with adventure" (Borges, 1964c: 44).

Debates in the field of reader-response criticism that emerged at the same time that Foucault and Barthes were writing about the author and the reader also questioned the degree to which the author controlled the meaning of the work, or asked whether the text or the reader were the source of meaning. Stanley Fish's discussions of reading are particularly interesting in the way they reverberate with Barthes's invitation that we embrace the text's plurality and acknowledge the reader's role as a creator of the text. In a headnote to the reprinting of his "Literature in the Reader: Affective Stylistics" he notes that his own essay was written in 1970 when Roland Barthes's *S / Z* "had just been published, and everyone was reading and talking" about it (Fish, 1980: 21). Fish's exploration of the reader was made first with respect to a particular text in *Surprised by Sin: The Reader in Paradise Lost*. Here Fish begins to suggest the reader's centrality. He argues that Milton's central strategy in this poem is to make the reader self-conscious about their own responses as a means of educating them. While the author is ostensibly still engineering these responses, the text's focus nevertheless shifts to the reader's textual experience. "[T]he poem's centre of reference" is therefore "its reader who is also its subject" (Fish, 1997: 1). His subsequent work extended the methodology he applied to this one poem to other texts and explored further the question of where meaning lies. On the one hand, he felt he was still adhering to formalist conventions against the "rank subjectivity" of positing the reader as the source of the text's meaning. But on the other hand, his work continued to displace the text's objectivity (the notion that it is simply *there*, as a self-sufficient and complete object) and to argue that the text was a spatial form "*actualized* in the temporal dimension by a reader" (Fish, 1980: 2). His essay "Literature in the Reader: Affective Stylistics" insists on the generative role of the reading subject who realizes the text through their reading experience (Fish, 1970: 125, 140). In his later formulation of the idea that the reader was part of an "interpretive community," Fish resolved the problem of the reader's response being wholly subjective, seeing it instead as proceeding from the interpretive community to which the reader belongs. Interpretive communities, he writes, "are responsible both for the shape of the reader's activities and for the texts those activities produce" since they implicitly regulate and condition acts of reading (Fish, 1980: 322). Still, this allowed Fish to retain the idea that "[t]here is no way of reading that is correct or natural, only 'ways of reading' that are extensions of community perspectives" (Fish, 1980: 16).

Recent discussions in cognitive narratology have similarly attended to the role of the reader, but examined it from the perspective of cognitive psychology and neuroscience as well as literary theory, analysing the mental processes of readers, and the way they respond to and make sense of a variety of narratives. There is less concern here with the subjective nature of the reader's response that so troubled Fish; and critics exploring the cognitive processes of reading vary between using a particular reader's responses (often their own) and studying the responses of multiple readers in order to make claims about them. In "*Don Quixote* and the Neuroscience of Metafiction," for example, Norman Holland is quite comfortable writing about his own experience of metafictional episodes in Cervantes's text, describing, for example, the "disconcerting effect" they have on him (Holland, 2012: 76–77); whereas Suzanne Keen's *Empathy and the Novel* utilizes collected readers' testimony (including her own) to assess the effects of their novel reading and to make arguments about the connections between their empathic responses and their actions in real life. Such focus on the way readers actualize the text they are reading tries to capture the malleable nature of the text and the results of the reader's mental processes.

Lisa Zunshine discusses precisely such mind-reading processes in *Why We Read Fiction*. Her work takes its point of departure from research on Theory of Mind to explore textual moments of "mind-reading," moments when the reader is called on to fill in what is missing from a text in order to make the narrative cohere.

We read fiction, she suggests, precisely *because* it engages such faculties in the reader (Zunshine, 2006: 162). Such cognitive approaches to reading may initially seem far off from Barthes's more theoretical calls for the primacy of the reader, and it is true that the disciplinary discourses of these two approaches are quite distinct. At the same time, reading Barthes from this contemporary perspective makes apparent just how much of his work, particularly in *The Pleasure of the Text*, is precisely an attempt to foreground the readerly experience: boredom, pleasure, incomprehension, bliss.

Finally, reading has become important to discussions of postcritique, described by Rita Felski as a term that refers

> to ways of reading that are informed by critique while pushing beyond it: that stress attachment as well as detachment, that engage the vicissi-tudes of feeling as well as thought, and that acknowledge the dynamism of artworks rather than treating them as objects to be deciphered and dissected.
>
> (Felski, 2017: 4)

Such attentiveness to the reader's experience of literature, that we also see in Philip Davis's *Reading for Life* (2020), seeks to find ways of talking about the reasons for which people are drawn to art (literature, painting, music, film) without construing them as naive. This is what Felski explores in her reassessment of the notion of readers' identification with characters in *Character: Three Inquiries in Literary Studies* (2019). Postcritique, she argues, seeks to find more "compelling vocabularies of value" to describe our interaction with artworks (Felski, 2017: 4). Similar calls to reconsider critical orthodoxies have been made by Sharon Marcus and Stephen Best in their discussion of "surface reading," which pointedly targets the metalanguages of psychoanalysis and Marxism and their process of "symptomatic reading" as respon-sible for assuming that an artwork's meaning is "hidden, repres-sed and in need of detection" (Marcus and Best, 2009: 1). Earlier suspicions of critique were voiced by Eve Sedgwick and her notion of a "paranoid hermeneutics" in *Touching Feeling* (2003), which itself echoes Paul Ricoeur's discussion of a "hermeneutic of suspicion" in *Freud and Philosophy* (1970). Using this term,

Ricoeur sought to characterize approaches that prize the unmasking or demystification of what is apparent. For him, this "school of suspicion" is dominated by Marx, Nietzsche, and Freud, all of whom are also scrutinized in contemporary discussions of post-critique (Ricoeur, 1970: 32). Such calls to rethink the role of hermeneutics can't help but recall Susan Sontag's 1964 essay "Against Interpretation," which characterizes interpretation as "reactionary, stifling" and calls for a criticism "which would supply a really accurate, sharp, loving description of the appearance of a work of art" (Sontag, 1982: 98, 103).

In *Revolution of the Ordinary*, Toril Moi points out that Eve Sedgwick wishes to make room for "reparative" reading alongside the usual "paranoid" or "symptomatic" or "suspicious" reading (Moi, 2017a: 176), and that what literary critics "call different 'methods of reading' are really different interests, and different views of what is important in literature (and life)" (Moi, 2017a: 179). Such themes are central to Ayşe Papatya Bucak's "Iconography," a story that reworks Franz Kafka's "The Hunger Artist." As Lucas Silver notes, both have a figure of a hungerer as their protagonist, and both authors explore the way people struggle to ascribe possible meanings to these two hungerers. Like Kafka's, Bucak's story suggests that the body of the hungerer (the surface meaning) and its significance (or hidden meaning) are not one and the same, and that meanings ascribed to these bodies are critical projections, ones that ignore the fact that the protagonist is not just a symbol but also a real, living being (Silver, 2021: 22). It is tempting for this reason to see Bucak's story as a parable of postcritique that displays the failure of a paranoic hermeneutics to attend to the artwork itself, to its surface meaning. Writing in intertextual relation with Kafka's work, Bucak's story refuses to ascribe meaning to the Starving Girl, thus foregrounding the problem of interpretation: "NEVER DOES THE STARVING GIRL think of herself as anything but hungry. It is the others who give her act drama, and meaning" (Bucak, 2019: 38).

We can see these various approaches to the reader at play in metafictional texts spanning the same decades in which interest in the author and in the reader arose. These texts question the authority of the author, as we have seen in works by Barthes and

Foucault discussed above, but also foreground questions about reception and interpretation through the figure of the reader. They foreground the reading experience to ask how we read and why, and attempt to describe the encounter with art. In the metafictional texts discussed in the remainder of this chapter, these issues are particularly prominent, insistent, and self-conscious. Having introduced some of the more salient approaches and discussions about reading and reception above, it is easy, for example, to see James Tate's "The Rally" as an exploration of interpretive communities, A. B. Yehoshua's *Mr. Mani* as reliant on the reader's mind-reading, or Ali Smith's *How to Be Both* as a work that examines our interactions with art along lines similar to those of writings on postcritique. What these metafictional works have in common is their insistence on an active and engaged reader, one who will pay attention, who is involved and aware of processes of meaning-making, and concerned with broad questions about art's meaningfulness.

THE READER IN (AND OUT OF) THE METAFICTIONAL TEXT

In the same years during which the role of the reader was being heatedly debated in literary theory circles, it was also centrally explored in fictional writing. Indeed, the reader figures prominently in contemporary metafictional works where three types of strategies towards representing, or addressing, or making specific demands on the reader can be discerned:

1　Metafictional works that centrally represent a reader on the diegetic level of the text, that is, in the narrative proper: an example of figural embedding seen in such texts as Julio Cortázar's "Continuity of Parks" and James Tate's poem "The Rally" discussed below.

2　Metafictional works in which the reader reading the narrative is addressed directly. In doing so, the narrative metaleptically crosses over to the extradiegetic level, to what lies outside the world of the told. Such works tend to exploit "the relational potential of the second-person pronoun" and gesture toward a metaleptic relation with the reader of the text that can be either momentary or sustained (McHale, 1987: 224–225). We have encountered such instances already, in *The French Lieutenant's Woman* and in John Barth's "Frame-Tale," where, respectively, the reader is chastised for believing in an omniscient narrator, or instructed to "cut … and fasten" the text in a particular way so to make it into a Möbius strip (Barth, 1988b: 2). Another example of such metafictional interpellation of the reader is Italo Calvino's *If On a Winter Night a Traveler*, which famously begins with the words: "You are about to begin reading Italo Calvino's new novel, *If On a Winter Night a Traveler*. Relax. Concentrate. Dispel every other thought. Let the world around you fade" (Calvino, 1981: 3). This gesture, interestingly, calls attention to the extradiegetic reader yet also asks that reader to enter into the text. An example of this metafictional technique can be seen in John Ashbery's metapoetic "Paradoxes and Oxymorons."

3   Finally, we see in recent postmodern writing a tendency toward texts that are structured in such a way as to call on the reader to engage in a variety of interpretive activities to consume the text: what Lisa Zunshine characterizes as moments of "mind-reading." These activities vary from requiring the reader to fill in information not provided by the text, to deciding in what order to read the contents of a text, to having the reader put together fragmented parts or separated sections of a work in the effort to make the novel cohere. At times such demands for readerly intervention might be explicitly stated, as in Cortázar's novel *Hopscotch*, which begins with a "TABLE OF INSTRUCTIONS" telling the reader that the novel can be read in two ways: in "a normal fashion" from chapter 1 to chapter 56, or by beginning with Chapter 73 and then "following the sequence indicated at the end of each chapter" (Cortázar, 1966). Three works discussed below that interestingly and explicitly call on the reader's cognitive skills to decide how to put the text together are A. B. Yehoshua's *Mr. Mani*, Geoff Dyer's *Jeff in Venice, Death in Varanasi*, and Ali Smith's *How to Be Both*.

READERLY PERILS IN CORTÁZAR'S "CONTINUITY OF PARKS" AND TATE'S "THE RALLY"

We might read Cortázar's story and James Tate's poem "The Rally" as cautionary tales about the experience of immersive reading. Cortázar's story begins with a man at his estate, sitting in an armchair reading a novel. Everything indicates that his reading experience is both pleasurable and immersive: "even the possibility of an intrusion would have irritated him had he thought of it" (Cortázar, 1967b: 63). He reads in the tranquility of his study, sprawled in his favourite green velvet armchair, after he has completed some urgent business. Effortlessly immersing himself in the novel, he "taste[s] the almost perverse pleasure of disengaging himself line by line from the things around him"; he subsequently enters the story he is reading yet more deeply, to the point of becoming a "witness" to the characters' actions: "word by word, licked up by the sordid dilemma of the hero and heroine, letting himself be absorbed to the point where the images settled down and took on color and movement, he was witness to the final encounter in the mountain cabin" (Cortázar, 1967b: 64). The lovers meeting in that cabin, meanwhile, are plotting to murder "that other body it was necessary to destroy" (Cortázar, 1967b: 64). One of them departs to commit the deed, the execution of which is also the point at which the story's two narrative levels (one telling of the man reading about the lovers, the other telling about lovers plotting a murder) merge: the lover runs to the estate, climbs up the stairs, then, knife in hand, reaches "the high back of an armchair covered in green velvet, the head of the man in the chair reading a novel" (Cortázar, 1967b: 65). Cortázar's condensed tour de force is both an allegory of reading and a cautionary tale. For, allowing yourself to enter a story to the point of detaching yourself from reality is one way of getting "killed off" by the text. Reading passively, a form of pure consumption, the reader in "Continuity of Parks" (and, likely, the reader of "Continuity of Parks") is also its victim, "that other body it was necessary to destroy." The cost of narrative pleasure and of uncritical immersion in literary texts in "Continuity of Parks" is high.

"There was some kind of rally going in the / common" we are told in the opening lines of James Tate's humorous poem, "The Rally" (Tate, 2004: ll. 1–2). The speaker decides "to drift over and check it out" (Tate 2004: ll. 4–5). In a way that is similar to Cortázar's tale, the text quickly sketches out the speaker's immersion: he mingles with the crowd (Tate, 2004: ll. 6–7), works his way toward the front, as the excitement is catching (Tate, 2004: ll. 16–17), starts to respond as one of the crowd (Tate, 2004: ll. 24–30), and acknowledges that the man speaking in the rally is "a powerful speaker" (Tate, 2004: l. 34). The meaning of what is being uttered, however, is entirely incomprehensible—both to the speaker and to us, the poem's readers. For the man's powerful speech includes such lines as "'I been down there where even the little / birdies fear to roam. I once found an angry viper / in my pocket, but steered the course. I bonged myself / with a hidden cloud'" (Tate, 2004: ll. 12–15) or "'[n]ever / before have we witnessed hairy hands with long fingernails / curl around the puffballs of history with such miraculous / dexterity'" (Tate, 2004: ll. 24–27). The speaker's incomprehension is contrasted with the crowd's understanding: they react to the words and contribute their own (also apparently nonsensical) responses. Meanwhile the speaker's attempts to interject his own enthusiastic phrases are summarily rejected. He yells "'Your duck just sat on a firecracker'" (Tate 2004: l. 21), at which point the man speaking at the rally pauses and tries to locate "the man who had spoken those words. / The crowd, too, / was looking around. I acted as though I were looking / also" (Tate 2004: ll. 22–25). Acting as part of the crowd, the speaker masks his outsider status. But in the poem's final lines, he makes a final effort to interpret the proceedings: "'What / happened to the pig?' I said. The man next to me looked / disgusted. 'There is no pig,' he said" (Tate, 2004: ll. 41–43). Though, unlike the reader in Cortázar's story, the speaker here is active, he nevertheless undergoes a similarly negative experience. Like Stanley Fish's interpretive communities we see here the way in which meaning is endemic to a particular group of speakers and listeners. Despite the humour of the poem, its more serious point is that meaning and meaningfulness are bounded by communal norms which also represent communal

boundaries. Despite the speaker's enthusiasm and desire to participate, meaning here remains inaccessible to those outside the interpretive community, illustrating the way readings "are extensions of
community perspectives" (Fish, 1980: 16). As in Cortázar's story,
Tate's poem enacts its ideas, making its readers experience the very
same pleasures, emotions, or frustrations as those of the reader /
speaker and implicating them in the power dynamics of reading and
interpretation.

METAFICTIONAL YOU'S

In "Continuity of Parks" and "The Rally" no explicit gesture or
address toward the reader is made. Rather, the presence of the
reader *in* these texts suggests directives or ideas for the reader *of* the
text by making them self-conscious about their own activities as
readers and about their own reading experience. This may entail
surprise, as in the ending of Cortázar's story, or confusion equal to
that of the speaker's own in Tate's poem. But metafictional works
often call directly to the reader using the second-person pronoun
"you," thus breaking down the divide between what is in the text
and what lies outside it, making the moment in which the text is
actualized coincident with the real time of the reading. One author
noted for doing so is the poet John Ashbery. His hallmark tactic is
not only to include a "you" in his poems, but often also to shift the
meaning and implications of this "you." The "you" in Ashbery's
poetry is an "elastic pronoun" (Vincent, 2007: 5). It might gesture
directly at the reader of the poem, but it may also be the speaker /
poet talking to himself (as in "My Erotic Double," "Just Walking
Around," or "And *Ut Pictura Poesis* Is Her Name"). Bonnie Costello, echoing charges against metafiction discussed at the beginning
of Chapter 1, argues that Ashbery's interest in the reader through
the use of the second-person pronoun saves his self-reflexivity from
becoming solipsistic (Costello, 1982: 493). But it is clear from the
poet's own statements that he is deeply interested in his audience,
that he "would like to please the reader." At the same time, he is
aware that, paradoxically, while being widely read he is little
understood (Ashbery, 2009: 179, 187). "You" handily signals
Ashbery's overtures to the reader and provides him with a means of

commenting on communication itself even as it sometimes also serves as, or ends up being, a way of talking to himself.

An early poem of Ashbery's titled "The Instruction Manual" shifts from a solitary act of conjuring up a visit to the city of Guadalajara (one the speaker imagines so as to avoid writing a dull instruction manual) to one that gradually invites the reader in. Midway through the poem, "you" appears alongside the invitation to join the speaker's revery: "Let us take this opportunity to tiptoe into one of the side streets. / Here you may see one of those white houses with green trim / That are so popular here. Look—I told you!" (Ashbery, 2008b: ll. 44–46). The gesture beckons the reader into the imagined city, making explicit the very process of reading as the process of entering into the world created by the author. At the same time, the poem's end reminds us that this city-vision—this space that is the poem—is just fiction:

We have heard the music, tasted the drinks, and looked at colored houses.
What more is there to do, except stay? And that we cannot do.
And as a last breeze freshens the top of the weathered old tower, I turn my gaze
Back to the instruction manual which has made me dream of Guadalajara.

(Ashbery, 2008b: ll. 71–74)

Ashbery's "The Instruction Manual" is an instruction manual for the imagination, a shared temporal experience with a reader that involves them both in flights of fancy and in the self-conscious awareness of the fictionality of fiction.

Ashbery's "Paradoxes and Oxymorons" even more centrally configures the role of the reader, not only using the "you," but also directly exploring the relationship between author, text, and reader. It begins by addressing the reader, lamenting the reader's inattentiveness, and the resulting failed communication between poem and reader:

This poem is concerned with language on a very plain level.
Look at it talking to you. You look out a window
Or pretend to fidget. You have it but you don't have it.
You miss it, it misses you. You miss each other.

(Ashbery, 2008d: ll. 1–4)

The poem has a message ("it") supposedly written plainly; but the reader's inattentiveness means that the poem's message and its reader somehow miss each other. Communication has failed. The message, as we read on, is perhaps not so "plain" after all—for "What's a plain level?" we may ask, and is there not also "play" in this linguistic system that makes meaning "open-ended"? (Ashbery, 2008d: ll. 6–11). The speaker continues, saying: "I think you exist only / To tease me into doing it, on your level, and then you aren't there / Or have adopted a different attitude" (Ashbery, 2008d: ll. 13–15). The speaker is motivated by the idea of the recipient and desirous of communication, despite knowing that understanding or even reception of the poem message is not guaranteed. Like Barthes's reader in *The Pleasure of the Text*, who distractedly reads, skips, looks up, drifts, and dips in again, the reader's attention cannot be counted on (Barthes, 1975: 12, 18, 24).

To this point, the speaker has ruminated *in* the poem about the various reasons why communication between poet and reader might be frustrated: the reader doesn't understand the poem or is distracted, the poem's supposedly plain level is not really so, the poet writes with the idea of a reader but then that reader isn't "there," or the message "gets lost in the steam and chatter of typewriters" (Ashbery, 2008d: l. 12). And yet, the poem also suggests in its final lines that some form of communication does occur after all. For "the poem / Has set me softly down beside you. The poem is you" (Ashbery, 2008d: ll. 15–16). Whether or not the reader has understood the poet or the poet has managed to address their actual reader, proximity and perhaps even closeness has been achieved through the act of writing and then reading. That the "poem is you" according to the poem's last sentence could have different meanings: that the text, absorbed by the reader, has merged with or become the reader; or that the reader, not the poem, is the central subject of the poem's imaginary. Either way, the text affirms the essential place of the reader in the text's production and meaning.

While Karin Roffman's biographical study of Ashbery has elucidated the possible personal context for the amorous-sounding discourse of this poem, the "you" in "Paradoxes and Oxymorons" speaks of a more general erotics of reading, one he shares with Barthes. The figure of the author, like the figure of the lover, is *"of an extreme solitude"* (Barthes, 1978: 1); and the author "must seek out this reader (must 'cruise' him) *without knowing where he is*" (Barthes, 1975: 4). Like Ashbery's "I think you exist only / To tease me into doing it" (Ashbery, 2008d: ll. 13–14), Barthes notes that, "It is not the reader's 'person' that is necessary to me, it is this site: the possibility of a dialectics of desire, of an *unpredictability* of bliss"; and from the point of view of the reader, he writes: "I *desire* the author: I need his figure ... as he needs mine" (Barthes, 1975: 4, 27). Ashbery's poems explore this act of communication, gesturing directly at the reader as an integral and essential interlocutor, "that *someone* who holds together in a single field all the traces by which the written text is constituted" (Barthes, 1977a: 148).

INTERPELLATING THE READER

Postmodern novels composed of different parts or perspectives make demands on their reader that realist texts do not. *Everything Is Illuminated* by Jonathan Safran Foer, for example, is made up of three different kinds of chapters: some comprise Jonathan's made-up history of his ancestors' shtetl in the Ukraine; some narrate the quest to find Jonathan's ancestral village from the perspective of Alex, son of the Heritage Tours Company's owner; some are made up of Alex's letters to Jonathan after their trip together in the Ukraine. Donal Ryan's *The Spinning Heart* (2014), recounting the economic collapse in contemporary Ireland through the lens of 21 different voices, similarly refuses to deliver a single coherent narrative. Here the reader must do the work of piecing together the various perspectives and stories in order to make sense of the narrative as one whole. An active reader is also called for in Geoff Dyer's *Jeff in Venice, Death in Varanasi*, a novel in two parts: the first takes place in Venice and is written in the third person singular, detailing the experiences of one Jeffrey Atman; the second written in the first-person singular recounts the narrator's gradual immersion into the city and culture of Varanasi. Is the protagonist of these two parts, one Jeff and the other "I," one and the same? Or, for that matter, is Jeff the character the same as Geoff the author? Is the story a continuous narrative of Jeffrey Atman's adventures as a journalist on assignment in Venice (in part one) and then on vacation in Varanasi (in part two)? Should we read the first as context to the second? Or are these two separate meditations on travel? In refusing to totalise the world of the text, these writerly novels turn the reader into a bricoleur, an active reader who must piece the various fragments of the work together, interpret them, and decide if and how they cohere.

A more extreme case of the reader as a necessary "writer" of the text can be found in A. B. Yehoshua's historical novel *Mr. Mani* (1989). Composed of five conversations with only one side of the conversation given, *Mr. Mani* forces its reader to reconstruct or imagine the words of the missing conversation partner. On the one hand, as Lisa Zunshine shows, such cognitive activity is one we engage with regularity when we read. But *Mr. Mani*'s structure more insistently lays bare and makes us aware of our cognitive functioning in the reading process. It also demands of its reader to be active. The following example from the first conversation gives a sense of how the reader's task in filling in the missing parts of the conversation varies and how it makes diverse demands on the reader's mind-reading:

—But what's wrong with that?

—Deceitful? Toward who?

—Not at all ... I'm sure Grandmother would be thrilled ...

—Something drew us there ... right into her bed ...

—No, not especially. I just thought it might interest you.

—Oh, I don't know ... maybe psychologically ... you must have some interpretation of it ...

(Yehoshua, 1992: 7)

The task of filling in the other side of the conversation is sometimes easy and sometimes uncertain; but regardless, in forcing the reader to imagine and resurrect it, Yehoshua turns his reader into an active producer of the text, making explicit the text's dependency on the reader's interpretive skills.

Ali Smith's *How to Be Both* (2014) resembles such works in offering up a novel made of two parts, both titled "One" (reminiscent of Susan Choi's *Trust Exercise* where the novel comprised three parts, all titled, like the novel, "Trust Exercise"). One part is situated in late twentieth-century England and focused on the adolescent George as she deals with her mother's death; together they had visited Ferrara to see the frescos of Francesco del Cossa. The other part of the novel is a first-person narrative by Francesco del Cossa, situated in Italy in the fifteenth century. Like Dyer's novel, Smith's asks its reader to consider how these parts fit together, but with the added challenge that it was published in two versions: in one of them, the fifteenth-century portion appears first; in the other, the twentieth-century portion appears first. Any reader purchasing the text or borrowing it from a library will unpredictably get one of these versions. The novel's structure and publication, then, asks us to consider not only how these parts fit together but also to consider the way that our understanding is determined by which of the two versions of the book we received and read. Having read the modern portion first, itself a matter of chance, do we read the novel differently than if we had gotten an edition that had the fifteenth-century portion first? And once we've read it one way, can we ever really read it otherwise? Even as the novel's title encourages us to embrace duality by labelling both parts "One," refusing to give priority to either part by not determining which comes first, reading's linearity must inevitably lend precedence to one part over the other. (Smith finds a different solution to the problem of the linear process of reading than the one given in *The French Lieutenant's Woman*, where the author figure's coin toss to determine which of the two endings will be narrated first is also an attempt to forestall the "tyranny of the last chapter, the final, the 'real' version," Fowles 1969: 406). Like the frescos described in the novel, we can see only the surface first and not the underdrawing beneath, not both at once. Yet, wonders George, "does that mean it comes first after all? And does that mean the other picture, if we don't know about it, may as well not exist?" (Smith, 2014: 89). In the Francesco portion, the artist similarly contemplates this troubling impossibility of not being able to experience both elements simultaneously, asking if there might not be some way "to tell a story, but tell it more than one way at once, and tell another underneath it up-rising through the skin of it" (Smith, 2014: 201). Such questions encapsulate the novel's own thematics, working in tandem to indicate the novel's very structure and to ask questions about interpretation, about what we see, and how we see.

Despite the impossibility of a fresco or a book conveying its dual nature, this novel does its best not to overdetermine the reader's sense of what comes first or what has priority by gesturing at or approximating simultaneity. A book in which everything could occur simultaneously is imagined by George as "one in which all the lines of the text have been overprinted, like each page is actually two pages but with one superimposed on the other to make it unreadable" (Smith, 2014: 11). The novel also gestures at this simultaneity in the George portion by depicting her mourning of her mother as a process in which the past (when her mother was still alive) and the present (in which she is dead) painfully co-exist. The novel, in fact, begins—if we have the George part first—with:

> Consider this moral conundrum for a moment, George's mother says to George who's sitting in the front passenger seat.
> Not says. Said.
> George's mother is dead.
>
> (Smith, 2014: 5)

This duality in the experience of mourning is one of the "both" of the title, as seen through the repetition of "says" and the corrective, past tense "said," as well as elsewhere in this part of the book where both presence and absence, past and present co-exist: "This will be the first year her mother hasn't been alive since the year her mother was born. That is so obvious that it is stupid even to think it and yet so terrible that you can't not think it. Both at once" (Smith, 2014: 6). In the fifteenth-century narrative, such simultaneity is conveyed by the contemporary and colloquial language of the Italian Francesco, whose language is peppered with contemporary phrases such as "just saying." And both parts of the novel play with gender, refusing to pin down the sex or sexuality of its protagonists. Thus the novel's structure as well as its content engage the reader in the materiality of the text: its limitations, its dualities and the implications these have for interpretation.

The brunt of the novel's metafictionality, beyond its structure and its mode of publication, is conveyed, however, through its discussion of visual art, offered as a model for reading. The experience of and response to visual art, in the George portion especially, explores questions of interpretation and models the process of experiencing art for the reader in a way that coincides with postcritical discussions about surface versus depth and about the viewer or critic's role in the interpretive process. The novel's postcritical stance has been noted by Elizabeth S. Anker and Cara L. Lewis who see its discussion of visual art as a means by which it conveys a general skepticism "about critique's relentless project of demystification" (Lewis, 2019: 132) and views the novel as one that "comes to interrogate and reject certain axiomatic interpretive assumptions," arguing instead for "a materialist, sensory, and embodied immersion in the experience of reading" (Anker, 2017: 20). We see the novel's questioning of interpretive strategies most prominently in George's description of conversations with her mother about the frescos of Ferrara. Initially, as George and her mother enter the palazzo's room of frescos, they simply gaze at them. George notes that the artworks are "so full of life happening that it's actually like life" (Smith, 2014: 44), while her mother "doesn't say anything. She just looks" (Smith, 2014: 48). Their subsequent conversation about the frescos turns to their context and to the identity of the artist, but the mother insists on just experiencing them: "it kind of doesn't matter, does it, that we don't know his name. We saw the pictures. What more do we need to know? It's enough just that someone painted them and then one day we came here and saw them. No?" When George offers to look the information up on the internet, her mother tells her not to, because "[i]t's so nice. Not to have to know" (Smith, 2014: 52).

This primal and unmediated encounter with art, however, is accompanied with other kinds of discussions about the works' symbolism, how this symbolism might indicate the sex of the artist, and the more general question of what comes first, "[w]hat we see or how we see?" (Smith, 2014: 90). In an exchange that confronts the reader with a psychoanalytic interpretative model of an artwork's latent meaning, George's mother notes certain shapes that suggest vaginal imagery and others that are phallic, concluding that the painter might have been female (Smith, 2014: 96). "Her mother did an art history degree once … and a women's studies degree," George notes, somewhat derisively, as she also registers that she was in the exact same room and "didn't see any of it" (Smith, 2014: 96). On the one hand, the mother insists on the primacy of looking at the artworks, but we also see her interpretive conditioning here by academia and its way of thinking about art, one distinct from the former pleasure of "surface reading." George's mother models both types of reading. She is not simply, as Anker claims, "a paragon of a theory-enamored literary critic," beholden to "a paranoic logic of double meanings that stifles and discounts crucial vectors of lived engagement" (Anker, 2017: 25, 33), but also models for George, and the reader, the pleasure of immersion of the experience of art that the novel seems intent on highlighting. That this is one of Smith's aims is made clear in the extensive and epiphanic description of George's experience of a painting of Saint Vincent Ferrer by Francesco del Cossa that she sees in a gallery after the family visit to view the frescos in Ferrara. This scene serves as the culmination of this portion of the novel. In it, George notes that "[i]t had taken a bit of looking to get past her own surface reaction to [the painting]" (Smith, 2014: 130). What is detailed over the next several pages is how George's looking process gradually unfolds after this initial "first look":

> At first … But then you notice … Then … That lets you start to see that … Then you notice that … Best of all … Or perhaps … Look at … Look at … George has become more and more interested in spite of herself and in spite of how little this picture—or any of the pictures in this room, all made more than five hundred years ago—seems on first glance to have to do with the real world. Now when she comes into Room 55, it's weird, but it's like she is meeting an old friend … *A friendly work of art.*
>
> (Smith, 2014: 132–135)

This deep absorption in and engagement with art—like calls for postcritical engagements with literature—foregrounds the importance of readerly pleasure and engagement and provides us with a vocabulary for describing immersion, enthusiasm, and affective responses to the work of art that gestures beyond what artworks "are meant to mean" (Smith, 2014: 152). The scene works to remind readers that, as Toril Moi has suggested, "literary criticism has no method other than reading," that "there is nothing special about our reading, except the attention, judgment, and knowledge we bring to the task" (Moi, 2017a: 5).

In this and other works discussed in this chapter, the reader or viewer's experience of the text or artwork is foregrounded and investigated. Through both form and content, these metafictional works engage us in thinking about the author and the reader. In attending to these figures and to the act of reception and interpretation, they enact or perform what they say about these essential questions about art, and force the reader / viewer to experience them firsthand. Exploring the "theory of fiction through the writing of fiction" (Waugh, 1984: 2) these works make us aware of our roles as readers and of the experience of reading. Doing so, they also ask us to consider questions that have long been the mainstay of literary interpretation: the extent of the author's authority, the question of the text's independent status, the role of interpretation, and the way in which meaning is produced. Most importantly, such works call on us to pay attention. They call out to us, pull us into the text, and force us to look and to think, to configure ourselves as part of the text's very fabric. They also remind us that producers of literature and producers of interpretation are doing much the same thing. In thematizing and exploring notions of the author and the creative process, and of the reader and the interpretive process, works like *How to Be Both* remind us of art's vibrant role and stake in art and in life. They tell us that our experience of art "would be this good" if we "devoted time to everything [we] looked at" (Smith, 2014: 133–134).

3

LUDIC METAFICTION
ON LITERATURE AND LANGUAGE GAMES

In the previous chapters we have seen examples of texts that consider and comment on such elements of fiction as narrative, narrative structure and style, or the figures of the author and of the reader. Some texts are metafictional not by commenting on such elements of fiction, but through their examination of language and its workings. Their consideration of language *is* their subject. Such texts are metafictional for several reasons: first, they comment on their own construction by discussing the very material out of which they are made; in this case, the material is not plot or characters but letters and words–that is, language. Second, their exploration of language's ability to refer to the real world is a means of questioning literary realism and of foregrounding the problems behind assumptions about language's referential function. Third, by highlighting the artifice that is language and by playing linguistic games with literary forms, such literary works question literary conventions and make them visible to the reader *as* conventions. Writers belonging to Oulipo (Ouvroir de littérature potentielle) invented new literary forms and revived old ones, and L=A=N=G=U=A=G=E poets self-consciously highlighted the

DOI: 10.4324/9781003180951-4

poem as a product of language. Their writings foreground both literary conventions and language to make visible the creative ways in which literary language can be playfully manipulated and deployed. They foreground, in other words, the artificiality of literary writing while expanding its repertoire. Finally, like other metafictions, works that foreground language and linguistic play use fiction to theorize about the use of language in fiction, thereby blurring the boundary between fiction and criticism. By systematically and self-consciously foregrounding language and language games, the works discussed in this chapter extend the linguistic experimentation of modernist writers like James Joyce and Gertrude Stein. They keep the reader from simply accepting the rules of grammar, and of literature, and in many instances foster creative engagement with lived experience beyond the text, as seen in such projects as *Subway Poems* and *Autonauts of the Cosmoroute*, discussed below.

The works explored in this chapter vary, but they all involve what Roman Jakobson describes as the metalinguistic function of language, one focused on the code of the communication itself, and they all problematize the referential function of language that is focused on language's denotative function. Where realism relies on the text's referential function, works that are predominantly focused on the metalingual function explore the "code" itself, asking questions about language's ability to signify, to communicate, and to convey information (Jakobson, 1978: 353–356). Works like John Barth's "Ambrose His Mark" and Lydia Davis's "Grammar Questions" investigate the adequacy of language to reality and to experience. Other works discussed in this chapter take a different approach to being anti-mimetic. They do so not by questioning language's ability to refer to the world, but by inventing new, formal literary constraints that play with literary conventions and highlight our awareness that all literature is a product of artifice. Through self-chosen and supplementary constraints, works like Lyn Hejinian's *My Life*, Georges Perec's *A Void*, Lydia Tomkiw's "Six of Ox Is," Christian Bök's *Eunoia*, and Walter Abish's *Alphabetical Africa* create new literary forms. Like other metafictional works, these problematize realism by thinking of literature itself as a pliant verbal construct and taking that construct as their explicit subject matter. Works like *Alphabetical Africa* and *Eunoia*, though written under rigorous, self-imposed constraints, nevertheless take a playful or ludic stance in their questioning of literary and linguistic conventions, and strive to remind us not only of the limitations of language or conventional literary forms, but also of their endless potential for invention and joy.

YOU CAN CALL ANYTHING ANYTHING

In a twist on Laurence Sterne's protagonist in *The Life and Opinions of Tristram Shandy*, who receives his name through a series of mishaps despite his father's attempt to use naming as a means of controlling his son's destiny, Barth's protagonist remains nameless till near the end of "Ambrose His Mark." Barth's is a story about how Ambrose got his name, about naming, signs, and language. Using the example of a proper noun, the story considers the arbitrariness of language and its weak and incomplete hold on reality. Signalling its side-stepping of conventional means of wedding name and thing, Ambrose's baptism is "delayed, postponed, anon forgot" (Barth, 1988a: 15). Meanwhile, the protagonist is referred to variously as "Christine" by his mother (because she had just seen Greta Garbo in *Anna Christie*), "*Honig*" (or honey in German, the family's national origins), or even "it." His Uncle Konrad holds out for *Hector* after the principal of the school he teaches at, and Aunt Rosa thinks that calling him *Thomas* might improve relations between grandfather (Poppa Tom) and grandson. Each of these possibilities circulate equally in the story's naming ecosystem. Tellingly, no paternal assistance in naming is to be had, as Ambrose's birth coincides with his father being committed to a mental institution. In this nod to Jacques Lacan's theorization of the paternal-linguistic function, Barth playfully indicates that there is no father here who can guarantee the Symbolic order (Lacan, 1977: 67). And no other traditions of naming provide definitive naming strategies either: the American Indians, says Uncle Konrad, name a child after finding out who he is; but Aunt Rosa counters his suggestion by saying that "some name their kids for what they want them to be" (Barth, 1988a: 17). In the first instance, identity determines the name; in the second, naming determines identity. Neither is asserted as the answer to the quandary of naming in this story, which aims to unsettle linguistic assumptions and conventions alike.

Signs or portents are not much help in the naming process either. When the conversation shifts from names to naming practices and finally to the port-wine stain on Ambrose's forehead as a telling sign of what his name might be, the uncertainty only increases. For the sign on Ambrose's forehead is *also* variously interpreted and debated, and provides no clear indicator of his destined moniker: a sign of brains (Barth, 1988a: 18) perhaps, or maybe "the devil's mark" (Barth, 1988a: 19), or perhaps a bee (Barth, 1988a: 31), the port-wine stain is an "ambiguous birthmark" (Barth, 1988a: 34). And yet, the "coincidence" of his nickname (*honig*), his birthmark, and his swarming by bees related near the story's end result in "Ambrose" becoming "by degrees" the protagonist's name despite the uncertainties of any clear sign: "It was to be my fate to wonder at that moniker," says Ambrose, "relish and revile it, ignore it, stare it out of countenance into hieroglyph and gibber, and come finally if not to embrace at least to accept it with the cold neutrality of self-recognition" (Barth, 1988a: 34). You can call anything anything, the story suggests; there is no inherent relation between word and thing. But it also argues that names, once assigned, come to designate gradually the entity they refer to: "Yet only give it voice: whisper 'Ambrose,' ... see what-all leaves off to answer! Ambrose, Ambrose, Ambrose, Ambrose! Regard that beast, ungraspable, more queer, pricked up in my soul's crannies!" (Barth, 1988a: 34). In this parable about the arbitrariness of linguistic signs, Ambrose and his sign are, finally, "neither one nor quite two" (Barth, 1988a: 34). They are not one because the connection between "Ambrose" and that being called Ambrose is not inherent in these entities. But they are also not two, because habit works to gradually link name and thing, to make Ambrose ineluctably "Ambrose." In this story, Barth is clearly using structuralist discussions of language inspired by Ferdinand de Saussure, who explored the relationship between signifier and signified in his *Course in General Linguistics*. Signifier and signified are the two aspects of the linguistic sign. They unite not word and thing, but sound-image and concept. Important for Barth's story too, is that the linguistic sign is itself something other than the referent, that thing in the world towards which language gestures (Saussure, 1959: 66–67). The case is of course different for proper names, where a sound-image is chosen to refer to an individual rather than established by convention. Barth focuses on this conundrum of naming, however, as paradigmatic, a means of underscoring the arbitrary link between word and concept, linguistic sign and thing.

Many of Lydia Davis's stories are metalinguistic to a greater extent than Barth's "Ambrose His Mark." In stories like "Grammar Questions" or "Example of the Continuing Past Tense in a Hotel Room," for example, the focus is squarely on the limitations and absurdities of language rather than on character or plot. These stories probe, as Jet McCullough has shown, the epistemological uncertainties that language cannot clarify, and express a skepticism about "the expressive and informative power of language" (McCullough, 2021: 1). At the same time, the very discussion of the limits of language yields a richer understanding of the ontological and psychological situations depicted in the stories even though the stories themselves do not veer from their insistent exploration of language. In "Grammar Questions" there is very little psychology to distract from the central question of how inadequately language is in describing experience. As in Grace Paley's "A Conversation with My Father" (discussed in Chapter 1), Davis's ground situation is the narrator's father's imminent death. Like Paley's story, Davis's works its way obliquely to this weighty subject matter, foregrounding instead language's inability to describe liminal states between life and death as well as the linguistic inaccuracies that attend our habitual language about the dead and the dying.

"Now, during the time he is dying," the story begins, "can I say, 'This is where he lives'? If someone asks me, 'Where does he live?' should I answer, 'Well, right now he is not living, he is dying'?" (Davis, 2007b: 27). The present participle, the narrator goes on to suggest, gives the false sense "that he is actively doing something" (Davis, 2007b: 28) just as the sentence "'He is not eating' sounds active, too. But it is not his choice. He is not conscious that he is not eating. He is not conscious at all" (Davis, 2007b: 29). At base, language here cannot give clarity with respect to ontological questions. Its grammar and its signifiers are incapable of providing exactitude with respect to liminal states such as that between living and dying; they often also mask the reality of death and the dead: "When he is in the form of ashes," asks the narrator, probing further, "will I point to the ashes and say 'That is my father'? Or will I say, 'That was my father'? Or 'Those ashes were my father'? Or 'Those ashes are what was my father'?" (Davis, 2007b: 28). At the heart of this story is the challenge of comprehending and perhaps coming to (linguistic) terms with the death of a parent, and, more broadly, with the ontological question of what it means to be. Questions about language and grammar bespeak the personal crisis while being unable to provide a satisfactory means of resolving it. At the same time, the story's questions are an effective means of representing the narrator's distress and, implicitly, the challenge of her acceptance of her father's death. The very limits of language here are also the limits of our ability to think about and to express non-being.

More humorously, other stories by Davis force the reader to consider language use by teetering on the verge of the nonsensical. Her short story "Example of the Continuing Past Tense in a Hotel Room" is composed of a notice, presumably from the hotel staff to their guest, indicating in the continuing past tense that the person in charge of cleaning their room "*has been* Shelly" (Davis, 2007a: 201). As in "Grammar Questions," we are asked to think about and acknowledge the impossibility of this statement whose grammatical correctness is nonetheless evident. The linguistic construction used in this very short story belies the housekeeper's sporadic or shadowy presence in the hotel room. It signals the absurdity of the hotel's claim of Shelly's continuous attentions, yet also suggests that one's comfort in the hotel room is indebted precisely to such absent figures as the housekeeper. In "Notes During Long Phone Conversation with Mother" the narrator notes that her mother needs a pretty dress made of cotton for the summer. But this reminder to herself quickly turns into a playful doodle, a visual rearrangement of the letters in the word "cotton" on the page, that ends with:

```
        toonct
   tocnot        tocont
   tocton
contot
```

(Davis, 2014: 101)

If the material of the would-be dress is cotton, the material of this story is language, here arranged and rearranged, not in order to create meaning, but to fabricate a different sort of textile. The story's initial mimetic situation is quickly displaced by its focus on linguistic play.

Davis's *Essays One* makes explicit her interest in language and underscores the thoroughness of her investigations, whether they involve jotting down all the permutations of letter order in the word "cotton" or probing for understanding of death and dying. "I like to understand things," she writes, "and tend to ask questions of myself or another person until there is nothing left that I do not understand" (Davis, 2019: 72). The various authors she discusses in her essay collection—Samuel Beckett, James Joyce, Bob Perelman, Edwin Morgan, Grace Paley, Louis Zukofsky, and Georges Perec among them—are of interest to her (as she says specifically with respect to Beckett) because of their "close attention to words, the mining of the richness of English, the ironic distance from prose style, the self-consciousness" (Davis, 2019: 7). Her own short stories draw on such self-consciousness with respect to language, and revise the form of the short story to accommodate this focus on the metalinguistic function of language. To the extent that for Jakobson, literariness results from our focus on the message itself in an act of communication—what he labels the "poetic function"—we might say that these stories by Davis ask us to accept the metalinguistic function *as* the poetic function. They force us to see language not only as that medium by which we refer to reality but as the material and subject of literature itself.

CONSTRAINT AND PLAY

The works discussed above by Barth and Davis ask their readers to think about language and representation, but they maintain a mimetic stance in so far as their characters and plots naturalize such questions: naming a newborn is indeed an exercise in ascribing a name to a thing or being, and the painful process of watching a parent die is one where one is likely to think about the ungraspable nature of the concept of death. The texts discussed below also highlight language, but might be described as "unnatural" narratives to the extent that they are written under specific and self-chosen constraints. Definitions of "unnatural narratives" differ. Jan Alber takes the "unnatural" in narrative as denoting some "physically, logically, or humanly impossible" scenarios or events regardless of whether these have been conventionalized in certain genres or not (Alber and Richardson, 2020: 8). Examples of such unnatural elements in stories include speaking animals or dead narrators (as in Pamuk's *My Name Is Red*). Brian Richardson, however, uses the term in a way that more pointedly addresses the conventions of literary realism. An "unnatural" narrative for him is one where events, characters, settings, or frames transgress or parody mimetic practices and are thus "anti-mimetic" (Richardson, 2015: 3–5). As will be shown below, literary works written according to a variety of freely chosen constraints—by Oulipo and other experimental writers—are anti-mimetic in the sense that they self-consciously experiment with the rules of language and literature rather than focus on these as a *means* of creating literary realist texts. Because they never allow their reader to forget the constructedness of their literary approaches, they insistently display how all language and all literature are, in fact, bound by conventions. They are not natural constructs. The formal and linguistic constraints that these works invent are always in addition to the constraints of the language the text is written in and to the constraint of genre and of literary forms. By self-consciously adding "pre-elaborated and *voluntarily* imposed systems of artifice," such writers underscore the constrained nature of textual production generally, and demonstrate that "all literature is fundamentally combinatoric in character" (Motte, 1986: 11; Motte, 2009a: 723). As Marcel Bénabou writes of Oulipian texts: they challenge the notion that a boundary exists "between two domains: the one wherein the observance of rules is a natural fact, and the one wherein the excess of rules is perceived as shameful artifice" (Bénabou, 1986: 41). Their short circuiting of the reader's ability to naturalize their understanding of language and literary conventions also force this same reader to participate in their linguistic and formal play.

Oulipian constraints are among the best known literary constraints. They were introduced by Ouvroir de littérature potentielle (Oulipo for short), a group founded in 1960 by Françoise Le Lionnais and Raymond Queneau that strove not only to invent new constraints but also to unearth constraints that, like the lipogram, had fallen into disuse. Language, of course, already entails constraints. And constraints on writing exist too. In writing a sentence, we must combine the words along a horizontal axis according to the rules of grammar (what Saussure called the *syntagmatic* dimension of language); and in choosing any one word within that sentence along a vertical axis, we must select one that is acceptable for that particular position in the sentence (what Saussure called the *paradigmatic* dimension of language) (see Culler, 1975: 13, or Sturrock, 1993: 24). Any sentence is thereby a complex combination of words along the horizontal (or syntagmatic) and the vertical (or paradigmatic) axes. But a constraint of the type used by Oulipo and others to produce literary texts involves a systematically applied supplementary rule that is self-chosen and is always more than convention (Baetens, 2012: 115). By inventing constraints or reusing past ones, Oulipian writers interestingly create a new approach to the avant-garde; they challenge the avant-garde notion of such anti-formalist practices as automatic writing or free verse by criticizing their ideal of formlessness as freeing. In what might seem initially to be a contradictory logic, central to proceduralism is the notion that extreme formalism "makes real freedom (i.e. invention, innovation, creativity) possible, whereas the kind of freedom that rejects rule-based practice or behaviour is condemned to remain at the threshold of invention" (Baetens, 2012: 120–121). Texts that operate by constraints effectively emphasize that writerly and readerly play is "an essential dimension of literary activity" (Motte, 2009a: 726), that creatively expands the realm of textual possibilities by inventing new forms and thus new experiences.

Some of these language experiments have been in poetry, by poets associated with the L=A=N=G=U=A=G=E magazine in the United States and by poets whose writing is sometimes language-centred. Some of these numerous language experiments include: an autobiographical work wherein the number of

chapters and the number of sentences within each chapter correspond to the author's age (Lyn Hejinian's *My Life*), a work
composed according to the principle of the Fibonacci number
sequence where each number is the sum of the preceding two, or
another wherein each section is focused on a letter of the alphabet
and explores the role of writing (Ron Silliman's *Tjanting* and *The
Alphabet*); a poem written entirely in palindrome (Lydia Tomkiw's "Six of Ox Is") or one tracing the narrative trajectory of
Tolstoy's protagonist in *Anna Karenina*, with each of its two parts
written in two word lines that sequentially follow the order of the
alphabet. The second stanza of this poem by David Lehman
titled "Anna K." begins with: "Afraid. Betrayed. / Can't divorce"
(Lehman, 2005: 42).

Such texts incorporate aspects of language or language theory
into the artistic work, or even, like Bob Perelman's *The Marginalization of Poetry*, blend academic criticism and poetry. The use of
language in these poetic works purposely seizes on language as an
external, non-semantically oriented system or order that works to
highlight and even prioritize the structure of language over personal
expression. It makes linguistic structures visible and impossible to
ignore, forcing the reader to consider language's structuration of
experience. Critical works by Roland Barthes such as *Roland
Barthes by Roland Barthes* and *A Lover's Discourse: Fragments*, like
Silliman's *The Alphabet* or Lehman's "Anna K.," also use the order
of the alphabet to question the coherence of the amorous and
autobiographical subject respectively. In *A Lover's Discourse*, the
arbitrary order of the alphabet is noted as a means of discouraging
"the temptation of meaning" and of keeping the fragments from
coalescing into a love story (Barthes, 1978: 8).

Other experimental literary texts work less to highlight the
arbitrary nature of language than to reveal the nature of literary
conventions that underly composition. Oulipian texts that create
texts by devising new constraints or by reviving constraints that
have fallen into disuse include such works as the following: Raymond Queneau's *A Hundred Thousand Billion Poems*, a book of
ten sonnets but with each line on a separate strip, such that a
reader can combine any one line with any of the others. Yielding
10^{14} or one hundred trillion sonnets, this work is an excellent

illustration of "potential" literature that, at the rate of reading "a sonnet per minute, eight hours a day, two hundred days per year," would take more than a million centuries to finish reading (Motte, 1986: 3). Queneau's earlier *Exercises of Style* retells the same story 99 times using a different style each time. Here, too, the notion of variation and permutation is used to proliferate a single sonnet or a simple and seemingly inconsequential story into an expansive text displaying multiple possibilities. Perhaps the most famous writing under constraint is by Georges Perec, another Oulipo member, whose novel *La Disparition* is written without once using the letter "e." Its sequel, *Les Revenentes*, is written *only* with the vowel "e." The translation of *La Disparition, A Void*, follows the same restriction as the original, necessitating, however, that it divert from the original: for example, Gilbert Adair's translation substitutes "six days" for "eight days" in the sentence that begins "Huit jours plus tard" (Perec, 2008: 25; and 1994: 11) because of the need for a number that does not contain the letter "e" in French (*huit*) or in English (six). "Eight," which would be the correct translation, would diverge from the work's lipogrammatic restriction. Many other interesting literary texts composed by Oulipian writers fill the pages of *All That Is Evident Is Suspect, Oulipo: A Primer of Potential Literature*, and Issue 22 of *McSweeney's*, a section of which is titled *New Work from Oulipo*. But non-Oulipian writers have also used the notion of constraint to create new and experimental works, five of which will be discussed below: Lyn Hejinian's *My Life*, Walter Abish's *Alphabetical Africa*, Christian Bök's *Eunoia*, Jacques Jouet's *Subway Poems*, and Julio Cortázar and Carol Dunlop's *Autonauts of the Cosmoroute*, the last two being works that take the exploration of literary constraints out into the world.

HEJINIAN, OR THE SUBJECT IN LANGUAGE

My Life, explains Hejinian in an interview with Dubravka Djuric, is intent on exploring "the relationship between social materiality and literary praxis." Her autobiographical project is political to the extent that it investigates how language is "saturated by ideology," and how one might block that system by "jamming [it] or by cutting the flow of communication" (Hejinian, 2000: 161–162). *My Life* does not entirely eschew a developmental model for the self in its efforts to disrupt flow, however: its reader will note a definite and gradual "shift from childhood to adolescence to adult thought and behavior" (Perloff, 1991: 162). A degree of coherence is also evident in the work's formal structure, which is directly linked to the life of its author. Written when Hejinian was 37 and revised when she was 45, the text restricts itself to 37 (and later 45) sentences per 37 (and later 45) sections. In addition, each section begins with a title phrase; the first is "A pause, a rose, something on paper." These italicized headings subsequently become refrains that are inserted at various points in the text, recontextualized each time they are uttered. For example, the title of the first section (*"A pause, a rose, something on paper"*) is repeated in the body of the third section, in the sentence "A pause, a rose, something on paper, in a nature scrapbook"; in the fifth section, where it appears as its own sentence; in the seventh section, where the sentence reads: "I found myself dependent on a pause, a rose, something on paper" (Hejinian, 2013: 8, 11, 16) and so on. The repetitions create continuity (if not coherence) and build up a series of associations with the phrase. Repetition, writes Hejinian, "disrupts the initial apparent meaning scheme. The initial reading is adjusted; meaning is set in motion, emended and extended, and the rewriting that repetition becomes postpones completion of the thought indefinitely" (Hejinian, 2000: 44). The repetitions alert the reader to the way in which the meaning of phrases or words change according to context. The phrase's local meanings can be parsed, and these meanings do accrue or become associated with the phrase in a logic internal to the work. Yet *My Life* refuses to fix their meaning, using them most prominently as leitmotifs or even purely melodic refrains. As the text suggests in a later section, "When you speak you play a language. The obvious analogy is with music" (Hejinian, 2013: 70). By suggesting that her reader consider language as creating continually malleable meanings or as creating pure sound, the repetition of phrases in *My Life* creates continuities while short circuiting semantics. In some sections, the frequency with which these headings are reused works to highlight the prefabricated nature of language itself, its existence prior to any particular instance of its usage and certainly prior to the auto-biographical subject. In this way, Hejinian creates a procedural structure while also questioning meaning and logic within this system. She also critiques the assumptions of autobiographical writing, discussed further in Chapter 5.

Jamming the system of language involves a variety of other techniques deployed in this work, such as the use of sentence fragments, semantic shifts or non sequitors, non-syntactical sentence structures, and a critique of conventional language such as clichés, turns of phrase, and metaphors embedded in the language (Hejinian, 2000: 187). Consider the following excerpt from the first section in which sequence is pointedly undermined while certain connections and associations are retained:

> I was afraid of my uncle with the wart on his nose, or of his jokes at our expense which were beyond me, and I was shy of my aunt's deafness who was his sister-in-law and who had years earlier fallen into the habit of nodding, agreeably. Wool station. See lightning, wait for thunder. Quite mistakenly, as it happened. Long tie lines trail behind every idea, object, person, pet, vehicle, and event. The afternoon happens, crowded and therefore endless. Thicker, she agreed. It was a tic, she had the habit, and now she bobbed like my toy plastic bird on the edge of its glass, dipping into and recoiling from the water. But a word is a bottomless pit. It became magically pregnant and one day split open, giving birth to a stone egg, about as big as a football. In May when the lizards emerge from the stones, the stones turn gray, from green. When daylight moves, we delight in distance.
>
> (Hejinian, 2013: 3)

The initial portrait of the aunt ends with "nodding, agreeably" and is only picked up again six sentences later with "It was a tic." In between this sequence are a number of disconnected sentences that seem to be the random expression of some consciousness; but they are disembodied, ascribed grammatically to no one. The discontinuity of the narration is neither a narrative in the normative sense, nor a stream of consciousness. The passage conveys thoughts, images, and ideas through apposition or parataxis, and presents the reader with a portrait of various family members while eluding normative progression or sequential development. Semantic shifts and shifts from concrete observations to abstractions keep the text from cohering (we mistakenly wait for thunder after lightning) even where an associative logic seems at play (as in the stone egg, which leads to the mention of the lizards' emergence from the stones). The reader is forced here to imagine the connective tissue that links sentences and thoughts: is "Wool station," perhaps, a reference to the knitting aunt? As in Barthes's notion of the open text, opened to plural meanings in the absence of its owner-author, Hejinian offers her reader ample space for creating connections or simply experiencing the text's capacity for disjunction. In the excerpt above, as everywhere else in *My Life*, Hejinian uses parataxis and reduces the syllogistic meaning of sentence sequences in order to increase ambiguity or polysemy. These are strategies and tendencies described in Ron Silliman's "The New Sentence" (Silliman, 1977: 91) and effectively summarized by Bob Perelman, who writes:

> a new sentence is more or less ordinary itself but gains its effects by being placed next to another sentence to which it has tangential relevance ... the internal, autonomous meaning of a sentence is heightened, questioned, and changed by the degree of separation or connection that the reader perceives with regard to the surrounding sentences.
>
> (Perelman 1993: 313)

Hejinian's focus on the unit of the sentence, her repeated use of certain sentences or phrases, and her intentional undercutting of syllogistic movement between sentences is a critical means of jamming the system of language in order to open it up for resignification.

Another means by which Hejinian sensitizes her reader to language and its way of making meaning is through her use of conventional or clichéd expressions. Her own, repeated section headings, among them phrases like "What is the meaning hung from that depend," "What memory is not a 'gripping' thought" or "I laugh as if my pots were clean," are, in a sense, her own created clichés. But she also directly tackles pat expressions in the language to signal its artificiality despite the subject's reliance on expressions as a means of expressing individuality. Again, her text moves nimbly from showing that subjects are constructed in language to revealing that they can also construct it. Speaking of "[her] grandmother," the speaker notes that she "had come upon a set of expressions ('peachy' being one of them and 'nuts to you' another) which exactly suited her, and so, though the expressions went out of everyone else's vocabulary, even years later, when everyone else was saying 'far out' or 'that's nowhere,' she continued to have a 'perfectly peachy time' on her vacations" (Hejinian, 2013: 12). While signalled as historically determined, "peachy" comes to define the grandmother's experiences. Other expressions, like "pretty is as pretty does" are integrated into the text so as to problematize their meaning, while other pat sayings are simply cut short, as in the sentence "Wild horses couldn't keep" (Hejinian, 2013: 3, 26). Towards the end of the text, the speaker yet more overtly asserts her oppositional stance, humorously asserting, "I do love to compare apples with oranges" (Hejinian, 2013: 92). Through these various means, Hejinian questions language as a coherent system capable of capturing experience or fixing the autobiographical subject. By disrupting grammar and syntax, questioning common or colloquial linguistic phrases, reducing language to sound, and subverting normative semantic progression through sentences, Hejinian forces her reader to feel the materiality of language and to participate in the process of making meaning that implicitly rejects authority, not only that of the writer, but also "the authority implicit in other (social, economic, cultural) hierarchies" (Hejinian, 2000: 43). Her use of form—that is, her structuring of this work through certain constraints—is a means of making "the primary chaos (the raw material, the unorganized impulse and information, the uncertainty, incompleteness, vastness) articulate without depriving it of its capacious vitality, its generative power." Form is, in other words, "not a fixture but an activity" (Hejinian, 2000: 47). *My Life* thus suggests simultaneously the determining and delimiting impact of language even as it reveals alternative views and, despite its formal restrictions, enacts the value of the open text. "The book," writes Hejinian, "is about the formative impact of

language, and at the same time it is a critique of that language—
suggesting that one can construct alternative views. *My Life* is both
determined and constructed. My life, too" (Hejinian, 2000: 187).

THE ALPHABETICAL WORLDS OF WALTER ABISH AND CHRISTIAN BÖK

The experience of reading Walter Abish's *Alphabetical Africa* is, like
the reading of *My Life*, revelatory with respect to language's
restrictions and effects. And like Hejinian's work, it is also an unnatural narrative in being both anti-mimetic and experimental. Like
other unnatural texts such as *Eunoia*, discussed below, *Alphabetical
Africa* is a kind of experimental fiction "that programmatically
transcends the paradigm of narrative" and undermines mimetic
reading strategies (Sommer, 2020: 95–96). First published in 1974,
this work is made up of 52 chapters, each titled with a letter following the sequence of the alphabet, first ascending from "A" to "Z,"
then descending from "Z" to "A." The first chapter ("A") only uses
words that begin with the letter "A." The second chapter ("B") adds
to these words that begin with the letter "B," and so on, adding
words allowed by the ascending order of the alphabet until the full
range of words beginning with any letter of the alphabet can be used
in the "Z" chapter of the first half of the work. The second half of
the book, conversely, begins with a chapter ("Z") in which any word
beginning with any letter can be used. The text then works its way
back to reducing allowable words, losing a permissible beginning
letter in each chapter until, once more, only words beginning with
the letter "A" can be used. Reading the entire work has the strange
effect of making the reader keenly aware of extreme linguistic constraints followed by a gradual naturalization of the narrative as one
nears the "Z" chapter. The expansion of permissible words through
the chapters leading up to chapter "Z" not only allows for new
places to be named (in chapter "E," suddenly, "Eritrea exists,"
Abish, 1974: 10) and new characters to appear; it also allows for the
inclusion of the first person singular in the "I" chapter. The first "I"
chapter begins with the sentence "I haven't been here before"
(Abish, 1974: 21) and the second "I" chapter closes with a reflection
on the I's impending disappearance: "Eventually, I'm convinced

every 'I' imparts its intense experience before it is erased and immobilized in a book. Ahhh ... how fast it disappears" (Abish, 1974: 131). The effect of the text is thus palpably to convey both constrained and naturalized language to the reader as it oscillates between anti-mimetic and mimetic modes; it makes obvious the ease of language without constraint and the strangeness of language with it. We forget to think so insistently about language (or constraint) in the middle chapters of the book and to note its severely limiting impact in the initial and concluding chapters. Along with naturalized language, the ascending chapters ("A" to "Z") correspond with "an increasingly coherent storyworld" (Sommer, 2020: 100) which then decreases in the book's second half.

While the actual content of the novel is focused on violence—particularly colonial violence—and the author's limited understanding of Africa given both his cultural and linguistic limitations (see Sainsbury, 2017), language *as* constraint remains its most dominant subject matter. In an interview, Abish has linked these two limitations, saying: the

> struggle to overcome the structural barriers I had devised for the text was my way of "controlling" and "dominating" a difficult text. Clearly there is a parallel between my struggle to depict and, as a white writer, come to terms with the "mysterious" of Africa and the intrinsic challenges of the text.
>
> (Abish, 1987: 19)

The prominence of the constraint's limitations is apparent from the very first chapter, and throughout the work are also strewn metafictional self-reflections on the nature of the work's composition. In the first "A" chapter, for example, the narrator comments metafictionally on the difficulty of "[a]pprehending Africa" and says: "author again attempts an agonizing alphabetical appraisal" (Abish, 1974: 1–2). Later, in one of many comments on the procedure of the text's composition, the narrator notes that he "has been losing a few letters each day" (Abish, 1974: 121), and makes the reader aware of which letters these are—either by highlighting the addition of new possibilities (always at the beginning of the ascending chapters) or the subtraction of certain possibilities.

In the first "E" chapter, we encounter the necessarily incomplete phrase "Easy come, easy ..." as words starting with "G" are not yet allowed (Abish, 1974: 11); and, later, in the second of the "Z" chapters, we read that Alfred, whose face has turned "a deathly chalk white" after eating zucchini, says to Alva: "Promise me ... that you'll never mention the word again" (Abish, 1974: 70). The text's language games, in other words, call attention to the writing process. Whereas Hejinian's work equally attends to language and to ideological concerns, the language games in *Alphabetical Africa* dominate its ideological, mimetic claims about Africa and coloni-alism. Such games with and about the constraint (and its con-straining effects for the author) call the reader's attention to the artificiality of both the writing and the reading process, thereby undermining a mimetic reading. It is not that unnatural narra-tives such as *Alphabetical Africa* call for unnatural responses on the part of readers; rather, they force readers to acknowledge "that narrative ... is not the only frame, or framework, that allows us to come to terms with literary fiction" (Sommer, 2020: 107). As in *My Life*, the wager of *Alphabetical Africa* is that writing under constraint is a means of creating new possibilities. Towards the end of the novel, the author figure notes: "I have always deleted in good faith, hoping I could find in completed book a far far distant happiness" (Abish, 1974: 128). He reminds us here of Hejinian's notion of the open text and its use of form and language not as fixtures but as activities that have the potential to turn "uncertainty to curiosity, incompleteness to speculation" (Hejinian, 2000: 41) and to foreground literature as a mode of inquiry.

In Christian Bök's *Eunoia* there is even less question of lan-guage as a means of referring to autobiographical subjects than in Hejinian's *My Life*, or to geographical spaces than in Abish's *Alphabetical Africa*. Here the constraint generating the text is that each of the five chapters of *Eunoia*—chapters A, E, I, O, and U— must restrict themselves to words with a single vowel. In order to create the work, Bök read *Webster's Third International Unab-ridged Dictionary* five times, extracting the lexicon of univocal words necessary to *Eunoia*'s construction and arranging them in ways conducive for composition (Bök, 2007). Various subsidiary constraints are described at the end of *Eunoia*, in an afterword entitled "The New Ennui," among them that

[a]ll chapters must allude to the art of writing. All chapters must describe a culinary banquet, a prurient debauch, a pastoral tableau and a nautical voyage. All sentences must accent internal rhyme through the use of syntactical parallelism. The text must exhaust the lexicon for each vowel, citing at least 98% of the available repertoire.

(Bök, 2009: 111–112)

Writing here is not triggered by notions of language's referentiality but inspired by the words and structure of formal expression. One might say that the dictionary is Bök's source of inspiration. Various political and social interpretations of *Eunoia* have interestingly explored the potential meanings of the text, arguing, for example, that the challenging constraints under which it works echo the experience of "living in seemingly inevitable plutocratic hegemonies" or that the poem teaches us that "vowels do have semantic overtones" (Marcoux, 2010: 89; Perloff, 2004: 36). But the work remains at heart a methodical linguistic exercise that explores what words can say at the very semantic limits of constraint. In an interview, Bök describes his procedure as one made to "determine what stories the vowels could tell," one resulting in his discovery that each vowel revealed an "individual personality." "Even under duress," writes Bök, *Eunoia* suggests that "language finds a way to express its own compulsions" (Bök 2007). Inspired by Oulipo, Bök has nevertheless written critically about the group's texts, saying that the results of their literary experiments often led to texts that seemed to resemble rote exercises because the "constraint often seems to take precedence over all other literary concerns" (Bök, 2005: 126). Like Oulipian works, however, *Eunoia* foregrounds its virtuosity, what Bök signals as the "Sisyphean spectacle of its labour" (Bök, 2009: 111). And like the texts written by other Oulipian or Oulipo-inspired writers, *Eunoia*'s enactment of constraint also ends up commenting on the nature and experience of that constraint. Like Abish's narrator who writes of his "alphabetical appraisal" or of "losing a few letters each day" (Abish, 1974: 1–2, 121), Bök's narrator-writer expresses the press of the constraint in *Eunoia*, as in the following meta-commentary in chapter "I": "Writing is inhibiting. Sighing, I sit, scribbling in ink this pidgin script. I sing with nihilistic witticism, discipling signs with trifling gimmicks–impish hijinks which high-light stick sigils" (Bök, 2009: 50). In chapter "E," the narrator ponders the book's reception, wondering about the book's engen-dering of "perfect newness ... even when vexed peers deem the new precepts 'mere dreck'" (Bök, 2009: 31–32). Works by Bök and Abish showcase the frictional relationship between language and expression. Working as they do under the press of limitations and at the limits of sense, their metalinguistic and metatextual com-mentary also effectively conveys the far-reaching effects that such language games might have on authors and readers alike: their encouragement of both playfulness and creativity within the bounds of the linguistically possible.

LIFE AND ART: CONSTRAINT ON THE MOVE

Wishing to incorporate play into lived experience, procedural writers have striven to transform the experience of everyday life practices through avant-garde artistic strategies, to blur the boundary between these two realms in order to infuse the every-day with the creative or political imperatives that their art galva-nizes. Daily life, that is, "should be *played*" in such a way that "game transforms quotidian experience through a kind of felici-tous alchemy, affording it a purpose and an aesthetic potential that it otherwise seems to refuse" (Motte, 2009b: 39). Examples of such practices, or what Michel de Certeau calls in *The Practice of Everyday Life* oppositional "tactics" (de Certeau, 1984: xxi) include Jacques Jouet's *Subway Poems* and Julio Cortázar and Carol Dunlop's *Autonauts of the Cosmoroute*. These works create a poem and a travel narrative, respectively, according to preset rules that are at once the means of creating the text and a proce-dure for travelling through real spaces. These rules are also devised as critiques of the restrictions and structurations of lived experience: not of language but of systems like the subway or the autoroute that, like language, control and delimit experience.

Going beyond existing conventions, they integrate artistic practice into lived experience with the purpose of re-enchanting such spaces as the subway or the autoroute, defamiliarizing them to create fresh texts and fresh perspectives on the worlds we inhabit. Here is how Jouet's poem describes its procedure (or game) of writing poems while riding the subway, linking writing and movement through the subway's stations:

> A subway poem is a poem composed during a journey in the subway.
> There are as many lines in a subway poem as there are stations in your journey, minus one.
> The first line is composed mentally between the first two stations of your journey (counting the station you got on at).
> It is then written down when the train stops at the second station.
> The second line is composed mentally between the second and the third stations of your journey.
> It is then written down when the train stops at the third station. And so on.
>
> (Jouet, 2001: 64)

Poem and lived experience coincide, evident in such lines as "The rhythm of days has now superimposed itself on the rhythm of stations" (Jouet, 2001: 67), which is simultaneously a line of poetry composed on the subway, and a reflection on the poetic practice that makes up the *Subway Poems*.

Such enactments of artistic play also highlight the political intent behind many of these practices, whether explicitly challenging capitalism (as in Silliman's "New Sentence") or the ideologies embedded in language (as in Hejinian's *My Life*), or implicitly challenging the norms and conventions of language and of writing. And, while some of the examples above have been characterized as "unnatural" or "anti-mimetic" narratives to the extent that they are not referential, works like *Subway Poems* by Jouet certainly seek to have an impact on reality by transforming their own experience as well as that of the reader, and by resisting the monotony of modern life. Julio Cortázar and Carol Dunlop's mock-epic journey from Paris to Marseille, *Autonauts of the Cosmoroute*, does so also. In what is surely an exemplar of "loiterature," this work practices delay and indirection as both sources of pleasure and a means of critiquing a culture of directness and speed (Chambers, 1999: 11). Instead of abiding by the autoroute's "monotony, obsessive time and space, fatigue" (Cortázar and Dunlop, 2007: 103), they explore possibility in its rationalized spaces. These "freewayistas" establish the following rules of the game:

1   Complete the journey from Paris to Marseille without once leaving the autoroute.
2   Explore each one of the rest areas, at the rate of two per day, spending the night in the second one without exception.
3   Carry out scientific topographical studies of each rest area, taking note of all pertinent observations.
4   Taking our inspiration from the travel tales of the great explorers of the past, write the book of the expedition (methods to be determined).

(Cortázar and Dunlop, 2007: 33)

What these rules yield is paradoxically a deep sense of freedom, of existing outside the autoroute's obsession with time and direction. The book charts Cortázar and Dunlop's experiences through mock-serious travel logs that detail their progress on the autoroute, record temperatures or what they consumed for each daily meal, note amenities at the various rest areas, and other incidental observations. But the text expands on such factual observations with more playful content: photographs, drawings, and ruminations on games, politics, time, art, love, and the genre of travel writing itself. The fictional characters Calac and Polanco from Cortázar's novel *62: A Model Kit* periodically make their absurdist appearances in several rest areas and in the text also, and fictional letters from a mother to her son in Canada tell of a strange couple she keeps seeing in the rest areas along the autoroute who seem "a bit happier than normal people" (Cortázar and Dunlop, 2007: 245). Explaining their presence to workmen who look at them in a funny way, they type furiously, telling them "that we're writing a book about the autoroute in order that they won't suspect what we're really doing: writing a book about the autoroute" (Cortázar and Dunlop, 2007: 204). Given such playful, imaginative games that *create* or remake the very space they are traversing, the question of Marseille's actual existence at the end of the journey seems uncertain, even spectral. Blending fact and fiction in their conclusion / destination, they write: "We won't prolong the doubt in the mind of our dear reader: Marseille exists, and it's just as Marcel Pagnol shows it. *But it only exists because the expedition has verified its existence*, and not for the reasons the masses accept, with no previous analysis" (Cortázar and Dunlop, 2007: 274). Upending any fixed ideas about the real and the imagined, *Autonauts of the Cosmoroute* teaches its readers to live creatively, even within the confines of a highly structured and rule-bound world. The text elucidates Oulipo's paradoxical claim that constraints produce play and generate unexpected possibilities, forms, and freedoms. The self-conscious reflections on language, artistic conventions, and generic norms that the works discussed in this chapter engage with, and especially their implicit questioning of limits and limitations, invite their reader to consider and to traverse the boundary lines between writing and living. Such work reminds us, as Daniel Levin Becker has said of Potential Literature, that "[t]o live your life craftily, whether you read it as a labyrinth or a puzzle or simply a long combinatorial succession of evenings and mornings, is to move through it with the purpose and the security that come from knowing you hold the tools to give it shape and meaning" (Becker, 2012: 318).

4

HISTORIOGRAPHIC METAFICTION
POSTMODERNISM AND THE HISTORICAL NOVEL

This chapter extends the question of referentiality discussed in the previous chapter to the historical questioning at the heart of historiographic metafictional texts. In the Introduction, metafiction was discussed as a departure from realism's assumptions about referentiality, and in Chapter 3, texts by John Barth and Lydia Davis were shown to explore language's inability to refer to the real world and its inadequacy in describing experience. Likewise, the postmodern historical novel examines our ability to represent and access the historical past. It asks questions about referentiality and historical truth, about the nature of our knowledge of the past and our access to it, and about the way narration of past events influences their representation and meaning in, and for, the present. Historiographic metafiction, a term coined by Linda Hutcheon in the 1980s, is a type of postmodern fiction that weds metafiction and historiography. Just as various definitions of metafiction have discussed it in terms of its departure from the style called literary realism, so historiographic metafiction has been discussed as a departure from the realist style of the classic

DOI: 10.4324/9781003180951-5

historical novel. Just as metafiction blurs the lines between fiction and reality, historiographic metafiction blurs the lines between fiction and history. It is predicated on arguments—on the part of both historians and literary critics—about similarities between literature and history that enable such blurring and questioning of the boundary between them. According to Linda Hutcheon, historiographic metafiction is fundamentally paradoxical. It takes historical contexts as significant but also problematizes them; it points to the problematic distinction between history and literature even as it makes use of this generic distinction; it questions and at the same time exploits the grounding of historical knowledge; and it offers a sense of the presence of the past even as it argues that this past can only be known from "its texts, its traces" (Hutcheon, 1988: 89, 113, 92, 125). Such contradictory impulses lead historiographic metafiction as described by Hutcheon to a "split politics," since it challenges received ideas but asserts nothing in their place (Elias, 2001: 88–89). Recent, twenty-first-century historiographic metafictions explored at the end of this chapter reveal, however, the political force with which these works address the past and its impact on the present, and the engagement with the past that these narratives demand of their readers.

This chapter will examine the concept of historiographic metafiction, both as a version and as a problematization of the realist historical novel, and discuss its historical and philosophical underpinnings. It will also note this concept's indebtedness to the work of historians like Hayden White and Keith Jenkins, who explore history's affinity with literature, particularly in its reliance on narrative and narrative tropes. Detailing the features and strategies particular to historiographic metafiction, this chapter will discuss how contemporary novels explore the complex nature of historical knowledge and its representation, returning to some texts discussed in previous chapters that demonstrate important aspects of this new type of historical novel (*The French Lieutenant's Woman, Flaubert's Parrot, Mr. Mani*), and examining new texts that illustrate important features of historiographic metafiction (*Possession, The Good Lord Bird, A Brief History of Seven Killings*, and *The End of Days*). The chapter will conclude by focussing more closely on two recent works of historiographic metafiction: Javier

Cercas's *Soldiers of Salamis* (2001) and Jonathan Safran Foer's *Everything Is Illuminated* (2002). These novels' sustained metafictions tackle the problem of accessing knowledge about the past, illustrated by their protagonists' quests: Javier's search for the man who saved the Falangist Rafael Sánchez Mazas from execution at the end of the Spanish Civil War, and Jonathan's search for his family history in Trachimbrod, a Jewish shtetl destroyed during the Holocaust. Like other metafictions discussed in this chapter, these merge the author and the protagonist figures, blurring the distinction between reality and fiction. But more centrally they tackle the question of fiction's relation to history, the textual nature of the historical past, and the role of narrative as a means of capturing, while also distorting, historical understanding. These metafictional texts investigate histories of conflict and oppression, and use metafictional devices to draw us into an empathic consideration of the past and its lingering effects on the present.

HISTORICAL AND PHILOSOPHICAL CONTEXTS OF HISTORIOGRAPHIC METAFICTION

While postmodernism is not the only period or style to question historical knowledge, or the epistemological underpinning of our access to historical facts, or the objectivity of recounting historical events, it signals a period in which such questions have been central (Hutcheon, 1988: 88). Historiographic metafiction arose in the context of the questioning of power and knowledge in the countercultural period of the 1960s, a period that saw the rise of colonial liberation movements and the ultimate collapse of the Soviet Block. Postmodernism is also a period of increased technological innovation that saw the inception of the World Wide Web and the rise of digital technology that influenced the cultural industry (Elias, 2016: 293–294). Historiographic metafiction also absorbed the themes and questions of poststructuralist theory that critiqued notions of truth, centre, and structure that had hitherto grounded the human and social sciences. These include Jacques Derrida's discussion of the "structurality of structure" and his critique of any fixed notion of a centre that limited play (see "Structure, Sign, and Play in the Discourse of the Humanities"); Michel Foucault's questioning of the notion of historical progress and of history as a stable structure derived by historians who saw their task to be the removal of discontinuity from history, and his attention to discourses themselves as constitutive of historical writing in such works as *The Archeology of Knowledge* and *Discipline and Punish*; Roland Barthes's argument that historical discourse is capable only of signifying the real, of creating a *"reality effect,"* because the discourse of history cannot reach the referent but only the signified (Barthes, 1989: 139); and Jean-François Lyotard's critique of the totalizing nature of metanarratives and of their problematic valuation as transcendent and universal truths (Lyotard, 1984). Interestingly, such theoretical questioning has led not only to new fictional forms like historiographic metafiction, but also to new critical approaches to literature like New Historicism in the US and various forms of cultural criticism in the UK and Europe. Developed by Stephen Greenblatt in the 1980s, New Historicism has amplified such poststructuralist and historiographic exploration in the social sciences by advocating an approach that avoids totalization, recognizes contradiction, and is self-conscious about its own historical methodologies (see Greenblatt's "Towards a Poetics of Culture"). Like Hutcheon, Greenblatt speaks of the past as accessible through its textual traces (Greenblatt, 1988: 4–7). As such, his cultural poetics' reconstruction of it is necessarily "fragmentary" (Greenblatt, 1988: 4). It is also inevitably determined by his own questions (Greenblatt, 2005: 5). Like the historiographic metafictions discussed later in this chapter, Greenblatt foregrounds "the impossibility of fully reconstructing and reentering" the past, and offers an historical practice that is self-conscious about both its findings and its limitations (Greenblatt, 2005: 5). These historical, technological, philosophical, and literary developments or trends have all contributed to a reconsideration of the mimetic relation between art and life in historical fiction, and have led to a new type of historical novel that uses distinctly experimental metafictional forms and techniques to ask questions about historical knowledge.

Literary theorists like Linda Hutcheon, Amy J. Elias, and Jerome de Groot, who have discussed historiographic metafiction, have been in intellectual conversation with the works of historians like

Hayden White and Keith Jenkins, historians who have discussed the status of history as a discourse and as a narrative about the past, who have written about the impossibility of reconstructing that past, and who have emphasized the ways in which "the past and history are not stitched into each other such that only one historical reading of the past is absolutely necessary" (Jenkins, 2003a: xiv). History, argues White in *Metahistory,* is "a verbal structure in the form of narrative prose discourse" (White, 1973: 2), one that in his subsequent essay, "The Historical Text as Literary Artifact," is explicitly likened to fiction: "*How* a given historical situation is to be configured," writes White, "depends on the historian's subtlety in matching up a specific plot structure with the set of historical events that he wishes to endow with a meaning of a particular kind. *This is essentially a literary, that is to say fiction-making, operation*" (White, 1978: 85, my emphasis). Upholding the importance of interpretive free-play, this questioning of the objectivity of historical knowledge, writes Jenkins, should not be taken as regrettable, but as an openness that "allows for new, disrespectful, contentious, radical readings and re-readings, writings and rewritings of the past ('the before now') to be produced" (Jenkins, 2003b: 3).

Such claims by historians are echoed by Linda Hutcheon in her initial formulation of historiographic metafiction as an experimental novel form she sees as capable of engaging with these important philosophical questions of the late twentieth century. Her articulation of this new form is clearly indebted to the kinds of questioning of historical truth expressed by White and to his blurring of the distinctions between history and fiction. She writes:

> The past really did exist. The question is: how can we know that past today—and *what* can we know of it? The overt metafictionality of novels like *Shame* or *Star Turn* acknowledges their own constructing, ordering, and selecting processes, but these are always shown to be historically determined acts. It puts into question, at the same time as it exploits, the grounding of historical knowledge in the past real. This is why I have been calling this historiographic metafiction. It can often

enact the problematic nature of the relation of writing history to narrativization and, thus, to fictionalization, thereby raising the same
questions about the cognitive status of historical knowledge with
which current philosophers of history are also grappling. What is the
ontological nature of historical documents? Are they the stand-in for
the past? What is meant—in ideological terms—by our "natural"
understanding of historical explanation?

Historiographic metafiction refutes the natural or common-sense
methods of distinguishing between historical fact and fiction. It
refuses the view that only history has a truth claim, both by questioning the ground of that claim in historiography and by asserting
that both history and fiction are discourses, human constructs, signifying systems, and both derive their major claim to truth from that
identity.

(Hutcheon, 1988: 92–93)

Hutcheon distinguishes here between the existence of the past
and its representation in the present, and proceeds, like White,
to detail the ways in which this representation is never neutral,
never simply factual. In linguistic terms, historiographic metafiction does not conflate the referent (the real) and the signified
(the idea or concept referred to); it reinstates the latter "while
at the same time not letting the referent disappear" (Hutcheon,
1988: 149). Her expression of historiographic metafiction's
profoundly paradoxical nature is not offered as a critique, but
as a means by which this new novelistic form remains vital,
open, and continually probing precisely by showing rather than
hiding the "ontological 'seams' between fictional projections
and real-world facts" (McHale, 1987: 17). Such literature "tries
to problematize and, thereby, to make us question. But it does
not offer answers. It cannot, without betraying its anti-totalizing
ideology" (Hutcheon, 1988: 231). Like Hutcheon, Brian McHale
also underscores the revisionary thrust of the postmodern historical novel, a novel that "revises the *content* of the historical
record, reinterpreting the historical record, often demystifying or
debunking the orthodox version of the past" and also "revises,
indeed transforms, the conventions and norms of historical fiction
itself" (McHale, 1987: 90).

FICTION AND HISTORY: SAME DIFFERENCE?

While historiographic metafiction draws on arguments about the similarities between history and fiction and while critics like Hutcheon view its effects positively, it is important to note that such rapprochement between history and fiction and the nature and effects of this postmodern type of historical novel have also been the subject of criticism. In his influential discussion of postmodernism, Fredric Jameson warned against the new flatness or depthlessness of postmodern art, its weakened historicity and effacement of the referent, leaving "nothing but texts" (Jameson, 1991: 6, 18). Most importantly, postmodern historical novels such as E. L. Doctorow's *Ragtime* "can no longer represent the historical past" but only our ideas and stereotypical representations of it. The genre of the historical novel survives, that is, but is "now emptied of its genuine historical content" (Jameson, 2013: 274). In an evocative passage that captures this notion of the lost historical referent, Jameson writes that we "can no longer gaze directly on some putative real world, at some reconstruction of a past history which was once itself a present; rather as in Plato's cave, it must trace our mental images of that past upon its confining walls." This new historical situation of postmodernism is one in which "we are condemned to seek History by way of our own pop images and simulacra of that history, which itself remains forever out of reach" (Jameson, 1991: 25). Whereas for Hutcheon, novels like *Ragtime* succeed in "making the reader aware of the nature of the historical referent" (Hutcheon, 1988: 89), they exemplify for Jameson the crisis of history and its attendant frustration of our ability to cognitively map our world.

Objections to the conflation of fiction and history have also been expressed in terms of their particular or distinct features, with respect to their referential claims, and in terms of the differing social contexts these two discourses occupy. As Lubomír Doležel notes in his discussion of Barthes's essay "The Discourse of History" and Hayden White's use of it in *Metahistory*, their interventions did not in fact make a significant impact on the Anglo-American historical profession (Doležel, 2010: 21). Philosopher Paul Ricoeur also counters White's claims about the similarities between fictional and historical narratives by arguing that, unlike fictional narratives, historical ones have the ambition "to constitute a true narrative," and the historian C. Behan McCullagh, while noting the importance of White's claims about historical narratives' literariness, similarly argues that historians "generally try to provide a fair overall representation of the central subject of their narratives" and that, in this sense, their narratives differ importantly from fictional ones (qtd. in Doležel, 2010: 22). The literary critic Dorrit Cohn also draws important distinctions between the fictional and the historical, writing that "referential narratives are verifiable and incomplete, whereas non-referential narratives are unverifiable and complete" (Cohn, 1999: 16).

More recently, the objection to the interchangeable use of the term fiction to describe both historical and literary texts has attended to the fact that they are differently situated in society and that narration, while applicable to both, is "not unique to literature but constitutes a real-life omnipresent mode of understanding, structuring, interpreting and transmitting real or imagined experience, knowledge, ideas and intentions" (Fulda, 2014). Fiction, according to Ansgar Nünning, has unlimited freedom to invent characters and narratives, whereas historical texts do not (see Fulda, 2014). Doležel similarly argues that historical works aspire to accurate reconstructions of the past that are "severely tested," and are restricted to depicting physically possible worlds (Doležel, 2010: 35–36). He also points out that historiographic and fictional narratives leave different types of gaps: historiography's gaps are epistemic and can be filled by the use or discovery of new sources or arguments, whereas gaps in fiction are ontic in nature, gaps created in their made worlds. These latter have to do with creating texts that "satisfy the human need for imaginative expanse, emotional excitement, and aesthetic pleasure" whereas historical texts "are constrained by the requirement of truth valuation" (Doležel, 2010: 37–38, 42). He does not disagree with Hutcheon's claim that "both historical and fictional representations of the past are semiotic constructs," but disagrees with her statement "that narrativization equals fictionalization" (Doležel, 2010: 90). The objections to arguments about the similarities between history and literature by Doležel, Ricoeur, Cohn, Fulda, and Nünning do not address the long-standing argument of whether it is the historian or the poet who, as Philip Sidney argued in "The Defense of Poesy" (1595), more powerfully rouses their reader or leads them to virtue (Sidney, 2000: 941–942). But as the discussions of historiographic metafictions below make clear, this issue is indeed a central concern for the authors and critics of such works.

Thus, fundamental questions must be asked by the reader of historiographic metafiction, namely: What type of historical or historiographic understanding do such novels facilitate? Do such novels suggest, as Hutcheon contends, that the past can only be known in its representations? Are there vital questions that historiographic metafiction is able to pose that historical narratives or the traditional historical novel cannot? And how do such novels position the reader (politically or affectively) vis-à-vis the past and the attempts to recuperate, reconstruct, and narrate it? One of the important aspects of the historical novel for Georg Lukács was its ability to provide a way of understanding the past by re-experiencing it, creating empathy in the reader by presenting characters that were the "living human embodiments" of "historical-social types" (Lukács, 1962: 27). Is this capacity to re-experience the past and to elicit the reader's empathic response still a mainstay in historiographic metafiction? Finally one must acknowledge that despite the importance of historiographic metafictions, literary realist historical novels of the type Lukács discusses continue to be written to this day, seen, for example, in Pat Barker's WWI novel *Regeneration*. Written in 1991, the "Author's Note" at the back of *Regeneration* strives to clarify and distinguish between fact and fiction, indicating to the reader "what is historical and what is not" (Barker, 1991: 335). And while including both fictional and historical characters in her novel, Barker clearly sees herself as adhering to strict historical truth in her depiction, noting that "it was always very important to me that I didn't change anything about the historical characters, that they actually thought and said what I've said they thought and did on a particular day" (qtd in De Groot, 2010: 104). In contradistinction, the historiographic metafictions discussed below, focus *in the text*, rather than paratextually, as in Barker's case, on the problems of historical reconstruction and narrativization. Despite their metafictional and postmodernist features, they too lay claims to such powerful effects as those evinced by the realist historical novel.

FEATURES AND STRATEGIES OF HISTORIOGRAPHIC METAFICTION

The following are some of the salient features and techniques of historiographic metafiction, each illustrated with reference to contemporary novels. They are the questioning of the historical record, the foregrounding of the enunciative situation that produces historical knowledge, the use of multiple viewpoints, the use of parody and intertextuality to complicate historical representation, the creation of an eccentric protagonist who views and narrates history from the sidelines, and the use of alternative histories that require the reader to question the past as well as to rethink issues of historical inevitability. No single novel contains all these features; but historiographic metafiction will make central use of one or more of them to problematize the representation of the past and to explore the generic boundaries between history and fiction.

(1) Historiographic metafiction highlights the failure or renders problematic the claims of the historical record. Rather than assimilate historical data into the fabric of the narrative, it foregrounds the *attempt* to do so. It thus self-consciously problematizes historical knowledge (see Hutcheon, 1988: 114; De Groot, 2010: 120).

Julian Barnes's *Flaubert's Parrot* illustrates this feature well in its second chapter, one made up of three distinct chronologies, each giving an entirely different perspective on the life of the writer Gustave Flaubert. The first underscores Flaubert's social, romantic and professional successes; the second chronology selects biographical details that render his life a tragic one, filled with the deaths of loved ones, illness, despair, and professional setbacks; the final chronology is made up of excerpts from Flaubert's own writings arranged chronologically. No chronological entry is factually inaccurate, yet each offers a different perspective on the writer and reveals how the selection and arrangement of historical data affects interpretation and meaning. That these three chronologies are arranged paratactically and are offered

without any mediating or explanatory commentary also underscores the need for the reader's interpretive involvement in any
construction of the historical record (Elias, 2001: 125–127).
Which is the correct version of Flaubert's life? the reader wonders. How might these disparate chronologies be unified into any
coherent whole? The historical record, Barnes demonstrates, is
selective and variable. It offers multiple, potential versions of
what happened that its reader must consider and interpret.

(2) Historiographic metafiction emphasizes its "enunciative
situation," focussing on the production of the historical record,
its reception, and the historical, social, and discursive contexts in
which reconstruction of the past occurs (Hutcheon, 1988: 115).
As we will see in the discussion of *Soldiers of Salamis* and
Everything Is Illuminated below, characters in such novels are
sometimes researchers, journalists, or otherwise interested parties
who seek historical knowledge about the past.

A. S. Byatt's *Possession: A Romance*, like John Fowles's *The
French Lieutenant's Woman*, weaves together action in the present
and in the Victorian past. Whereas Fowles's novel contextualizes the
Victorian age from a variety of disciplinary perspectives, particularly
through the use of epigraphs, Byatt's novel focuses on the literary
world. Her novel details the work of various literary critics in their
attempt to reconstruct the life and work of two Victorian poets:
Randolph Henry Ash and Christobel LaMotte. Archival discoveries
and the interactions of various literary scholars foreground the ways
our understanding of the past is mediated by accidental findings, the
interpretive biases or predilections of scholars, and the institutions
that enable their work. The novel juxtaposes, for example, the work
of those associated with the English Professor Blackadder, those
associated with the rival American Professor Cropper's research
team, and the work of North American feminist scholars like Leonora Stern. While Blackadder and Cropper largely follow traditional historical-textual methodologies, predicated on a cult of the
male author and the fetishization of all objects connected to him,
the feminist scholarship of Dr Maud Bailey and Leonora Stern, and
the deconstructionist methods of Fergus Wolff differ distinctly in
their understanding and writing about the life and works of the
Victorian authors in question.

We witness the way in which each scholar possesses different information and ideas about the past, and the novel's focus on a trove of hitherto unknown letters between Ash and LaMotte affirms not only the way in which our understanding of the past is reliant on archival evidence available at any point in time, but also the way in which such evidence revises past understandings of the historical record. The found letters require the "need to reassess *everything*" (Byatt, 2018: 577). We follow Roland Michell and Maud Bailey as they make their discoveries, ones that will overturn established scholarship and affect the lives of the various scholars involved in this enterprise. Unlike the writer at the centre of *Flaubert's Parrot*, the Victorian poets Ash and LaMotte are fictional characters. Byatt herself composed the poetic works quoted at length in *Possession*. She thus not only proposes in this novel that the past is discovered, produced, received and discursively con- structed according to differing ideological, interpretive perspectives, and serendipitous discoveries, but emphasizes that point yet further in choosing fictional poets and their fictional work as the basis of this drama.

(3) Historiographic metafiction is often composed of multiple points of view, a form that implicitly undermines the notion of a single historical truth. Through such multiple viewpoints, the text suggests the various potential perspectives on the past, as exem- plified in Byatt's *Possession*. It also turns the reader into "the actualizing link between history and fiction, between the past and the present" (Hutcheon, 1984: 228).

An interesting recent use of multiple viewpoints is found in Marlon James's *A Brief History of Seven Killings,* which tells the story of the 1976 attempted assassination of Bob Marley, and, more broadly, depicts Jamaica in the turbulent decades of the 1970s and 1980s. Anything but brief at nearly 700 pages, this novel represents this period of Jamaican history through 12 different narrators that, together, thematize the complexity of neo-imperialist, masculinist, and transnational violence reverberating through Jamaica and the Jamaican diaspora. These various narrative viewpoints also utilize different genres or styles to evoke the far-reaching effects of national and transnational violence: gang crime fiction, Cold War spy fic- tion, and New Journalism (Walonen, 2018: 2–3). Together these multiple perspectives and styles suggest the complexity of Jamaican history in the age of globalization and decolonization and gesture at the multiple, transnational channels of violence that are part of the island's postcolonial history. As one of the novel's epigraphs, a Jamaican proverb, suggests, this history can only be approximated: "If it no go so, it go near so" (James, 2014).

(4) Historiographic metafiction uses intertextuality and parody (an imitation of a previous text) to suggest that a sense of the past can only be created out of texts or traces, that the past is accessible in textualized form alone (Hutcheon, 1988: 129, 125).

Byatt's own composition of a variety of invented intertexts written by her invented Victorian poet-protagonists, Ash and LaMotte— letters, diaries, poems, and prose fiction—pose as "authentic" texts of the Victorian period in *Possession*. They combine, as Doležel notes, with a great variety of other kinds and styles of writing (notably literary criticism) to form a "textual collage" (Doležel, 2010: 100) depicting the encounter between the contemporary and the Victorian period. Fowles's approach to representing the Victorian age in *The French Lieutenant's Woman* differs somewhat from Byatt's; rather than create those past texts himself, and, in so doing, both parody and naturalize this past, *The French Lieutenant's Woman* uses actual authorial interventions to both resurrect and question the nature of the past thus revived. The novel quotes extensively from Victorian sources, or sources that themselves quote Victorian sources, in order to depict the age. As in Byatt's novel, these are from diverse genres and disciplines: many are literary, but others are historical, sociological, economic, scientific, philosophical, or anthropological. Together, these texts paint a portrait of the Victorian period and highlight the fact that our access to the historical record is textual in nature. At the same time, the narrator-author figure in *A French Lieutenant's Woman* overtly questions his own relationship to the historical material and narratives he quotes, offering different ways of understanding his own fascination with the period: "So perhaps," writes the narrator-author in chapter 13,

> I am writing a transposed autobiography; perhaps I now live in one of the houses I have brought into the fiction; perhaps Charles is myself disguised. Perhaps it is only a game. Modern women like Sarah exist,

and I have never understood them. Or perhaps I am trying to pass off a concealed book of essays on you. Instead of chapter headings, perhaps I should have written "On the Horizontality of Existence," "The Illusions of Progress," "The History of the Novel Form," "The Aetiology of Freedom," "Some Forgotten Aspects of the Victorian Age" ... what you will.

(Fowles 1969: 95, ellipses in the text)

Fowles's genius in this novel is his raising of historical self-consciousness about both the Victorian and the contemporary periods. His novel's intertextuality and parodic historicity simultaneously restore and question past and present, and offer its reader a series of interpretive possibilities ("perhaps ... perhaps ... perhaps") for reading the text in which this very relationship between past and present is so insistently evoked.

(5) Rather than having a protagonist who represents an historical type, as in the realist historical novel, the protagonist of a historiographic metafiction is often ex-centric, a marginalized or peripheral figure of fictional history (Hutcheon, 1988: 113–114).

James McBride's protagonist in *The Good Lord Bird* is a good example of just such a peripheral figure, as "Onion" finds himself on the sidelines, tagging along with the abolitionist John Brown and witness to his 1859 raid on Harpers Ferry. As in Byatt's *Possession* and Mat Johnson's *Pym* (discussed in Chapter 1), the premise of James McBride's novel is the discovery of a manuscript that overturns established historical knowledge. In *The Good Lord Bird*, the found manuscript is a memoir by one Henry Shackleford, a former slave. It seems to have been gathered and recorded by a member of the First United Negro Baptist Church of the Abyssinia named Charles D. Higgins, an amateur historian. We are told that the congregation "has announced plans to pass the account of Mr Shackleford to a Negro history expert for verification" (McBride, 2013: 3). Like Johnson's Chris Jaynes, or Byatt's Roland Michell, McBride's protagonist is a minor player and an outsider to power and knowledge. Shackleford is taken for a girl in his accidental meeting with the abolitionist John Brown in a Kansas tavern, then nicknamed "Onion," and later rechristened by Brown as "Henrietta." Conscripted into John Brown's army and taken along by him as a good luck charm, Onion is privy to important historical events. Through the eyes of this cross-dressing young African-American protagonist we learn of Brown's preparations and subsequent raid on Harpers Ferry, and we meet important historical figures like Frederick Douglass and Harriet Tubman, all comically and irreverently rendered from Onion's sideline, naive perspective. Through the character of Onion the novel both reproduces and disrupts historical representation of the period and its main actors (see Ahad-Legardy, 2021: 51–52).

Like Huckleberry Finn, to whom McBride's Onion has been compared, Onion's perspective is granted important insights about identity and race, and about historical figures like John Brown. He is able to have access to Brown, and to see the inside workings of Brown's abolitionist efforts and idiosyncratic personality. His marginal position, as both a slave and a girl, allows him to traverse boundaries, and he draws insights from such experiences. He realizes at one point, for example, the similarities between racial and gender oppression and reflects on the nature of identity, saying:

> I'd gotten used to living a lie—being a girl—it come to me this way: Being a Negro's a lie, anyway. Nobody sees the real you. Nobody knows who you are inside. You just judged on what you are on the outside whatever your color. Mulatto, colored, black, it don't matter. You just a Negro to the world. But somehow ... I come to the understanding that maybe what was on the inside was more important, and that your outer covering didn't count so much as folks thought it did, colored or white, man or woman.
>
> (McBride, 2013: 318)

The peripheral or ex-centric protagonist of historiographic metafiction, that is, may be on the sidelines, but nevertheless serves as an insightful point from which to reflect on broad and important issues.

Onion's own peculiar vantage point and the way in which this "single subjectivity [takes] precedence over any of the major issues that 'History' produces" has led critic Gerald David Naughton briefly to wonder whether the novel is "posthistorical" (Naughton, 2018: 354)—that is, as not in fact interested in history. But Naughton proceeds, rather, to suggest that McBride's novel maintains an engagement with history despite contesting the historical record and suggesting that it is incomplete. He also notes that the novel is "scrupulously researched ... carefully woven around the established history of the Harpers Ferry raid" (Naughton, 2018: 350, 351). The very foregrounding of Onion's idiosyncratic position and the way in which the historical events of the novel are inflected by the identity confusion of its protagonist-narrator are themselves a common element of historiographic metafiction, in which history remains a very real concern. That Onion's idiosyncratic position is given such precedence, forcefully proposes a reconsideration of historical knowledge in this novel. Indeed, McBride's thorough historical research prior to writing *The Good Lord Bird* led him to reconsider the trustworthiness of historical sources and their ability to tell "the whole truth" (McBride qtd. in Naughton, 2018: 350). With its off-centre protagonist, *The Good Lord Bird* is able to explore the historical record, to speculate about its various lacunae, to irreverently question some of history's sacred cows, notably in its depiction of Frederick Douglass, and to draw on subjective lived experience as a source of insight for history's inner workings. Masquerading as Henry Shackleford's historical memoir, the novel traverses the boundaries of history and fiction to question, explore, and destabilize historical certainties.

(6) Finally, historiographic metafictions often offer alternative histories, filling in debates about, or lacunae in, the historical record with speculative versions of what happened, or what might have happened.

A. B. Yehoshua's *Mr. Mani*, for example, offers us an alternative vision to the ethnic, cultural, political, and religious divisions and animosities that define modern-day Israel. It moves backwards in time through five sections, thus peeling away the layers of historical inevitability. Each section is located at a historically significant and different moment, among them the aftermath of the 1982 Lebanon War, the Battle of Crete in 1941, and the Balfour Declaration in 1917. We see in the first conversation (set in 1982) the deeply divided and fractious landscape of modern-day Israel through a representation of Jerusalem and its inhabitants. But as we proceed into the past, we encounter a different kind of city altogether: multi-ethnic, multicultural, and multilingual. It is a city in which different identities coexist and mingle, a city that is "still a collection of uncollated ideas," a city where "[e]verything is jumbled together" (Yehoshua, 1992: 368, 365). Yehoshua has described the aim of the novel thus: "In its contrary progression, it not only indicates junctions at which historic options were missed, but in the literary dream it weaves it also attempts to emancipate all of us and heal us from facts that occurred" (Yehoshua, 2001: 1). The novel's syncretic, multi-ethnic Jerusalem is offered up both as a critique of nationalist consolidations that took place over the course of the 19th and 20th centuries, and as an ideal or model for a radically multicultural state. Likewise its formal devices, such as reverse chronology, one-sided conversations, repetition among its various disjunctive parts, disrupts and complicates models of identity and of nationality (see Hoffman, 1992: 255). Indeed, the novel's title, one that underscores the centrality of the Mani family, is made up of a surname that means "who / what am I?," opening up the question of identity rather than asserting any national, political, cultural, or religious essence.

More recently, Jenny Erpenbeck's *The End of Days* builds its historical narrative from the telling of the fate of one character living through the turbulent twentieth century. In each of the five books that make up this novel, the protagonist, unnamed till the end, dies at a different point in time: in Book I, she dies as a baby in Galicia under the Austro-Hungarian Empire; in Book II she dies as a result of suicide in Vienna at the end of WWI; in Book III she is a victim of Stalin's purges, and, accused of being a Trotskyist spy, her life ends in a forced labour camp in 1941; in Book IV she is an accomplished author in East Berlin and dies from an accidental fall down the stairs of her home; finally, in Book V, the now-named Mrs Hoffman dies shortly after her 90th birthday in a united Germany. Between these books, Erpenbeck inserts "Intermezzo" sections that question historical inevitability: what if she hadn't turned the corner and met the young man who then drove her to suicide? What if Comrade F had put her file on the right-hand pile rather than the left-hand pile? The conditional perfect tense dominates these sections where Erpenbeck traces the life of her protagonist's trajectory against the historical upheavals that determined it only to suggest again and again that "things might also have gone quite differently" (Erpenbeck, 2012: 167). Like Yehoshua, Erpenbeck uses her novel to question historical inevitabilities and interpretations.

Erpenbeck's novel's title echoes Francis Fukuyama's post-Cold War essay in which he had notoriously suggested that we may be "witnessing the end of history as such," having reached the culminating point of human evolution in the form of Western liberal democracy (Fukuyama, 1989: 4). Erpenbeck suggests otherwise. We see this questioning of historical interpretation pointedly in the description of Mrs Hoffman's son's experience in Vienna:

> The border that used to separate him from the West has long since fallen—but now it seems to have slipped inside him, separating the person he used to be from the one he's supposed to be now, or allowed to be... And he couldn't care less if the others can tell by his way of looking around, by his hair and cheeks, that he comes from the land that has finally, rightly so, thank God, high time now, been wiped off the face of the earth, the land of—what madness—publicly owned enterprises, red carnations for your lapel on May 1, rigged elections, old men wearing berets left over from the Spanish Civil War, and dialectics taught at school.
>
> (Erpenbeck, 2012: 223)

The novel refuses any definitive end to history in its critique of capitalism and liberal democracy. Instead it strives to examine the complex interweaving of historical and personal scales, to question any definitive linear narratives, and to forestall notions of happy endings in favour of historical questioning. "I don't know," are Mrs Hoffman's last words "what it can mean that we are so sad" (Erpenbeck, 2012: 237). Much of the novel's poignancy comes from the sense of a lost past rather than a triumphant present.

THE HOLOCAUST AND SPANISH CIVIL WAR THROUGH HISTORIOGRAPHIC METAFICTION

Javier Cercas's *Soldiers of Salamis* and Jonathan Safran Foer's *Everything Is Illuminated* are both quest narratives in which the protagonists seek historical knowledge respectively about an event during the Spanish Civil War and about a Ukrainian shtetl wiped out during the Holocaust. These texts illustrate well Hutcheon's point that the discursive affinities and similarities between literature and fiction do not mean that there is no truth of the past. While the past may be accessible only through texts, subjective or partial witness accounts, and while it may exist in fragmented or conjectural form in these works, the task of the narrators is to discover as much as they can about it. The novels devise complex structures in order to foreground the search and the precarity or incompleteness or impossibility of historical knowledge, and in order to provide the reader with a sense of the questions, disagreements, and problems that underwrite the creation of any historical narrative. At the heart of both novels lie two historical unknowns: the impossibility of reconstructing the life of the Jewish Shtetl of Trachimbrod given its utter destruction during the Holocaust, and the impossibility of ever ascertaining who protected the Falangist writer Rafael Sánchez Mazas from the firing squad and why that individual did so. Indeed, both novels insist on a kind of vicious circular logic that characterizes the relationship between the desire for historical knowledge and any final or satisfactory understanding of history: "I couldn't stop thinking about Sánchez Mazas," says the narrator of *Soldiers of Salamis* who is named, like the author, Javier Cercas. "I soon arrived at a conclusion: the more I knew about him, the less I understood him; the less I understood him, the more he intrigued me; the more he intrigued me, the more I wanted to know about him" (Cercas, 2020a: 53). Crucially, these novels locate the desire to know in the present, emphasizing that the quest for historical truth involves not just the question of establishing the historical record, but also the legacy and effects of that past in the present.

"TRUE TALES" OF THE SPANISH CIVIL WAR

"True tale" (*un relato real* in Spanish) is an often repeated phrase in Javier Cercas's *Soldiers of Salamis*, one that immediately problematizes the boundary between non-fiction and fiction, between history and literature. Cercas's work has been animated by an intense exploration of this boundary, as can be seen in the titles, subtitles, and subjects of his works: His 2000 short story collection is titled *Relatos Reales*, or *True Stories*; his 2014 work, *The Imposter*, examines the life of Enric Marco, a respected veteran of the Spanish Civil War and an activist Holocaust survivor who was exposed as a fraud in 2005, a man who literally invented his biography and who, for a long time, operated in society as if that invention were fact; and his most recent work to be translated into English, *Lord of All the Dead*, which is subtitled "A Nonfiction Novel." The narrator of *Soldiers of Salamis*, a journalist who has also published fictional narratives, insists frequently that he is writing a "true tale" about an incident that took place during the Spanish Civil War when the Falangist Rafael Sánchez Mazas escaped a firing squad and managed to flee into the forest due to the decision of an unknown Republican soldier not to give him away. Fascinated by this story and seeking to comprehend and discover both the motivation and identity of this soldier, Javier, distinguished in my account from "Cercas," the book's author, insists to all who will listen that he is not writing a novel but a "true tale": it is "like a novel," he explains to his girlfriend. "Except, instead of being all lies, it's all true" (Cercas, 2020a: 75). Cercas has occupied this blurred generic terrain between truth and lies for much of his career, and *Soldier of Salamis* squarely places its reader along that disquieting boundary line. The novel insists that its reader read it as a "true tale" and uses this mongrel generic designation to dramatize questions about the distinction between history and fiction: What part does invention play in the writing of history? In a situation where the historical record is incomplete or contradictory, can we fill it in with invention? And where exactly does fact turn to invention in the interpretive process of gathering historical evidence?

The novel's very structure both describes the process of historical research and interpretation and enacts it, its three parts detailing the historical quest and constructing different narratives about it in turn. In the first part, the narrator tells of the first time he heard the story of Sánchez Mazas, in 1994, when he interviewed his son, Rafael Sánchez Ferlosio. But it is only in 1999, during the sixtieth anniversary of the end of the Spanish Civil War that he recalls the story of Sánchez Mazas's botched execution. He writes an article titled "An Essential Secret" that retells both the tragic end of the Spanish poet Antonio Machado on the French side of the France-Spain border, and adds to it "a kind of chiasmus of history" (Cercas 2020a: 20–21) in the story of Sánchez Mazas's escape from death on the Spanish side, near the Sanctuary of Collell. But this article is just the starting point of Javier's fascination with this story. What follows is a dizzying, detailed account of his subsequent search: interviews, archival research, film viewing, and the reading of many additional sources that corroborate the story's main outline but also provide somewhat conflicting information. From the 82-year-old Daniel Angelat's telling of his encounter with Sánchez Mazas, Javier first hears of that Falangist's plan "to write a book about all that" and to call it *Soldiers of Salamis* (Cercas, 2020a: 81), information that proves crucial to his own telling:

> The next day, as soon as I got to the newspaper I went to the editor's office and negotiated a leave of absence.
> "What?" he asked ironically. "Another novel?"
> "No," I answered smugly. "A true tale."
> I explained what I meant. I explained what my true tale was about.
> "I like it," he said. "Have you got a title yet?"
> "I think so," I answered. "*Soldiers of Salamis*."
>
> (Cercas, 2020a: 82)

Self-reflexively, reiterating the novel's title, part two provides the reader with this very "true tale," predictably titled "Soldiers of Salamis." Part 2 is thus a *mise en abyme* of the text as a whole that, for a second time, and with much additional detail, retells the story of Sánchez Mazas and his escape from the firing squad at Collell.

Part two—the "Soldiers of Salamis" embedded within the *Soldiers of Salamis*—offers a longer narrative of what transpired, but one still filled with historical uncertainties. In further proliferating the levels of narration and the number of stories about Sánchez Mazas, part two also has the effect of complicating the relationship between reality and representation further: Is Javier the same individual as Cercas? Is the "Soldiers of Salamis" a doubling of

Soldiers of Salamis? Whose book and what narrative is the reader reading here? Added to this are the uncertainties voiced in this second version of the Sánchez Mazas story. For, despite purporting to provide us with the complete historical narrative, part two repeatedly signals the incompleteness of Javier's historical reconstruction, filled as it is with such phrases as:

"What follows is not what actually happened, but rather what seems probably might have happened." (100)

"[T]he truth of this version could well be called into question." (101)

"There are those who maintain that ... Another version ... There even those who claim ... However it happened, the truth is that ..." (106–107)

"It is possible that ..." (120)

"I don't know if time has given the scene a novelistic varnish; although I can't be sure, I tend to think not ..." (136)

"[S]ome allege that ... Others maintain that ... There even those who ..." (152)

"This version of events is reliable, to my mind ..." (153)

"[T]here are some who suspect that ... The conjecture is attractive, but false" (156)

In short, there is much that is still conjecture, up for debate, unknowable. Part two of the novel initially seems to offer more knowledge and more detail, but, like the fissures in Javier's first attempt, his commemorative essay about the Spanish Civil War reproduced in part one, it too proves inconclusive. More than that—or so part three indicates—"Soldiers of Salamis" or part two of *Soldiers of Salamis* is decidedly unsatisfactory; initially "very pleased" with his finished work, Javier's reading and rereading of it yields disappointment. Part three begins with this overwhelming sense of the narrative's insufficiency. Despite his efforts to revise and reorder it, something is still missing:

> I read it euphorically; I reread it. At a second rereading my euphoria gave way to disappointment: the book wasn't bad, but insufficient like a mechanism that was whole, yet incapable of performing the function for which it had been devised because it was missing a part. The worst of it was I didn't know what part it was. I revised the book thoroughly, I rewrote the beginning and the conclusion, I rewrote several episodes, I rearranged the order of others. The part, however, did not appear; the book remained hamstrung.
>
> (Cercas, 2020a: 166)

Herein, of course, lies the dual function of part three: on the level of the book as a whole, it supplies that missing part, which is of course this last part of the novel; but more specifically, and more narratively, it supplies a proper hero to the firing squad story in the figure of Miralles, whose story is told to Javier by his friend, the author Roberto Bolaño. One of Líster's soldiers who had followed him through Catalonia, Miralles, thinks Javier, may be the very soldier who saved Sánchez Mazas at Collell: "I heard myself murmur, in the pitch-black silence of the bedroom: 'It's him'" (Cercas, 2020a: 191). Later he tells Conchi, his girlfriend, Miralles's story, insisting that "Miralles (or someone like Miralles) was exactly the part that was missing in order for the mechanism of the book to function" (Cercas, 2020a: 194–195). Javier now begins his search for Miralles despite Bolaño's protestations that he should make him up because the real Miralles would only disappoint him (Cercas, 2020a: 197). Interestingly, this last quest for the "missing part" (or gap) problematizes Doležel's distinction, discussed above, between epistemological and ontological gaps as a means of distinguishing between history and fiction respectively. Both such gaps are at play in the "true tale" according to *Soldiers of Salamis*; both are important in the writer's consideration of incompleteness. For a satisfactory historical narrative or true tale, this text argues, is one that strives to fill in epistemological gaps *and* ones that have to do with its world making.

In this final and, indeed, most moving part of the novel, we meet Antonio Miralles, a former Republican soldier now in his 80s and living in the Nimphéas Residential Home in Fontaine-lès-Dijon. Though he denies being the soldier who saved Sánchez Mazas's life, he nevertheless functions as the hero hitherto missing from Javier's book, the hero whose memories and valour during the Spanish Civil War the novel revives. The novel concludes having resolved its structural, political, and even personal conundrums through the figure of Miralles. Structurally Miralles supplies the work with a proper hero, not only by becoming that soldier who perhaps saved Sánchez Mazas, but also by possessing, precisely in his unassuming way, the qualities of a hero. The text suggests that politically Miralles provides a preferable model to Sánchez Mazas, a Falangist author who won the war but whose talent as a writer was never realized (Cercas, 2020a: 161), a writer who, in his paradise of "chintz and slippers" illustrates that "writing and plenitude are incompatible" (Cercas, 2020a: 162); and personally, Miralles offers Javier, still mourning the death of his own father since the summer of 1994, the year he first heard about Sánchez Mazas facing the firing squad, a kind of substitute father figure. In the novel's conclusion, relating Javier's thoughts as he takes the train from France back to Spain, these various levels converge, creating a masterful metalepsis that weaves in the various narrative threads of *Soldiers of Salamis* and collapses the novel's various spatio-temporal planes into a single, self-begetting narrative:

> I saw my book, whole and real, my completed true tale, and knew that now I only had to write it, put it down on paper because it was in my head from start ("It was the summer of 1994, more than six years ago now, when I first heard about Rafael Sánchez Mazas facing the firing squad") to finish, an ending where an old journalist, unsuccessful and happy, smokes and drinks whisky in the restaurant car of a night train that travels across the French countryside ... while he thinks of a washed-up man who had courage and instinctive virtue and so never erred or didn't err in the one moment when it really mattered, he thinks of a man who was honest and brave and pure as pure and of the hypothetical book which will revive him when he's dead.
>
> (Cercas, 2020a: 245–246)

Javier's vision of his book and its conclusion *is* the book's vision and conclusion in this narrative about the legacy of the Spanish Civil War, about the challenges of reconstructing the historical record, about the process of writing, and about the demands of "true tale" narratives. The reader of *Soldiers of Salamis* may remain uncertain about some historical facts or of where precisely the boundary between fiction and history lies, yet becomes aware throughout the course of the narrative of the processes through which writings about the past are derived and shaped, and of the contexts and conditions in which, and because of which, this same past is revived and written in the present.

SEARCHING, WRITING, AND READING IN FOER'S *EVERYTHING IS ILLUMINATED*

Everything Is Illuminated shares with *Soldiers of Salamis* important metafictional elements in its exploration of the Holocaust, ones that blur the line between fiction and reality and make the space of the novel simultaneously a space where its historical concerns, modes of narration, and specific contents are discussed and debated. Self-reference and self-commentary, narrative embedding, and doubling (e.g. of the author Jonathan Safran Foer and the protagonist Jonathan) continually obscure and problematize the boundary between what is fictional and what is real. Like *Soldiers of Salamis*, Foer's 2002 novel is also a quest narrative in which Jonathan travels to the Ukraine, intent on finding his family's ancestral shtetl, Trachimbrod, and writing a book about it. His only clue is a "yellow and folded" photograph depicting his grandfather Safran with a family who, Jonathan presumes, saved his grandfather from the Nazis. On the back of the photograph, written in Yiddish, are the words: "This is me with Augustine, February 21, 1943" (Foer, 2002: 59–60).

As in Cercas's novel, discussion of the relation between knowledge and invention is central to *Everything Is Illuminated*. At the same time it is made more palpable and unsettling in Foer's novel. This is partly because this novel does not settle on any generic designation, such as the "true tale," but continually presents the reader with three different and alternating modes of narration: Alex's narration of the quest to find Trachimbrod and Augustine; instalments of the novel Jonathan is producing after the trip to the Ukraine and which he is sending to Alex; and Alex's letters to Jonathan, detailing his reactions to Jonathan's novel. Each of these portions expresses, though in different ways, the incompleteness of the historical record; and each fails to provide certainty or plenitude: Alex's narrative of their experiences in the Ukraine is told through his peculiar and sometimes approximate grasp of the English language, and, in his letters to Jonathan, he admits that he embellishes his narrative, sometimes (see for example Foer, 2002: 54, 142) in order to make it humorous or in order to please Jonathan; Jonathan's novel is a magical realist representation of shtetl life, from its founding, when Trachim's wagon "did or did not pin him against the bottom of the Brod River" in 1791, to its tragic end on 18 March 1942 (Foer, 2002: 8–13, 267–73). It is replete with impossible and fanciful details and imbued with a tragic sensibility. In it he invents the life of his grandfather Safran in the absence of concrete historical knowledge; finally, Alex's letters to Jonathan are but one side of a correspondence that leaves us guessing about the content of Jonathan's letters to Alex. His final letter encloses his grandfather's suicide note, which ends in an unfinished sentence using the future tense (Foer, 2002: 276).

In addition to its structural foregrounding of invention, unreliability, and incompleteness, the novel concertedly dramatizes the necessity for the creation of narratives about the past that results from absence, from finding nothing. Like Cercas's novel, Foer's too signals the inverse relationship between knowledge and invention in passages that refer to Jonathan's recording of the trip in his diary: not only does Alex note, upon seeing Jonathan writing in his diary, that "[t]he less we saw, the more he wrote" (Foer, 2002: 115), he also notes Jonathan's indecision about whether to record what is occurring at all (Foer, 2002: 154), or even his decision not to hear any more painful testimony about the shtetl's demise (Foer, 2002: 186). Yet Foer's novel is more insistent than Cercas's about the impossibility of knowing, dramatized repeatedly in its emphasis on silences, holes, nothing. For starters, "Augustine"—or the woman they find and whom they initially believe to be Augustine—is all that is left of Trachimbrod: "You are here. I am it," she tells Jonathan, Alex, and Alex's grandfather (Foer, 2002: 118). Her house is filled with strangely labelled boxes that contain the shtetl's fragmented remains: labels such as WATCHES / WINTER, SILVER / PERFUME / PINWHEELS, DARKNESS, SLEEP / SLEEP / SLEEP, and the box labelled IN CASE that "Augustine" gives Jonathan (Foer, 2002: 147–150, 192). This strange and bizarrely catalogued archive signals the fragmented history of the Jewish village as well as the difficulty of reconstructing its history. Their subsequent arrival in Trachimbrod is equally bewildering: though "Augustine" tells them, "We are here," Alex's narration describes a place where

> [t]here is nothing. When I utter "nothing" I do not mean there was nothing except for two houses, and some wood on the ground, and pieces of glass, and children's toys, and photographs. When I utter that there was nothing, what I intend is that there was not any of these things, or any other things.
>
> (Foer, 2002: 184)

A commemorative historical plaque marking the shtetl's destruction is all that remains. It reads:

THIS MONUMENT STANDS IN MEMORY

OF THE 1,204 TRACHIMBRODERS

KILLED AT THE HANDS OF GERMAN FASCISM

ON MARCH 18, 1942.

Dedicated March 18, 1992.

Yitzhak Shamir, Prime Minister of the State of Israel

(Foer, 2002: 189)

Most poignantly, it is Alex's letters to Jonathan, ones that comment on Jonathan's novelistic instalments, that forcefully thematize the problem of invention given the lack of historical documentation. They also try to digest and give meaning to the revelation that the past actions of Alex's grandfather, who turns out to be a contemporary of Jonathan's grandfather, led to the death of his Jewish friend Hershel. This is where the novel centrally comments on fiction, and on the role of narrative not only as a means of reconstructing the past, but also as a means of affecting the future. In his letters, Alex increasingly disapproves of Jonathan's tragic retelling of Trachimbrod's history, insisting that writing gives second chances (Foer, 2002: 144). In a letter dated 12 December 1997, he writes:

> We are being very nomadic with the truth, yes? The both of us? Do you think that this is acceptable when we are writing about things that occurred? If your answer is no, then why do you write about Trachimbrod and your grandfather in the manner that you do, and why do you command me to be untruthful? If your answer is yes, then this creates another question, which is if we are to be such nomads with the truth, why do we not make the story more premium than life? It seems to me that we are making the story even inferior. We often make ourselves appear as though we are foolish people, and we make our voyage, which was an ennobled voyage, appear very normal and second rate. We could give your grandfather two arms, and could make him high-fidelity. We could give Brod what she deserves in the stead of what she gets. We could even find Augustine, Jonathan, and you could thank her, and Grandfather and I could embrace, and it could be perfect and beautiful, and funny, and usefully sad, as you say. We could even write your grandmother into your story. This is what you desire, yes? Which makes me think that perhaps we could write Grandfather into the story. Perhaps, and I am only uttering this, we could have him save your grandfather. He could be Augustine. August, perhaps. Or just Alex, if that is satisfactory to you. I do not think that there are any limits to how excellent we could make life seem.
>
> (Foer, 2002: 179–180)

Alex's letter underscores not only the absence of truth, but the narrative choices possible in its absence. This is what *Everything Is Illuminated* does also, in detailing the disappointments of its historical quest and in depicting Jonathan's and Alex's different ways of writing about the past. Jonathan's and Alex's sensibilities not only differ here; we are also shown how they are differently positioned vis-à-vis the past and how they are shaped by it, how that experience affects them in the present and how it leads to their divergent narrative choices. That Foer's novel refuses to conclude by settling on any one version of the past—tragic or comic—makes of this novel an exploration and a questioning of historiography and of the familial experiences that underwrite the relationships between history and fiction.

In *Succeeding Postmodernism*, critic Mary Holland suggests that twenty-first-century postmodern works like *Everything Is Illuminated* wrestle with poststructuralist questions about language, narrative, and truth to create new kinds of realist narratives, ones that solve these problems from within poststructuralism, and use metafictional devices to create empathetic and humanist texts (Holland, 2013: 3). Such texts achieve these aims "not by repressing the machinations of fiction, as does traditional realism, but by making them visible via metafiction"; they use metafiction and anti-realism "to remind us of the powerful ways in which acts of reading and writing impact the real world" (Holland, 2013: 7). Recent historiographic metafictions like Foer's and Cercas's construct novels around novels and histories around histories not just to problematize the past, but to engage their readers in the affective repercussions of the past as it reverberates in present lives. These post-postmodern works, as Holland refers to them, go beyond metafictional games for their own sake

> to salvage much-missed portions of humanism, such as affect, meaning, and investment in the real world and in relationships between people, while holding on to postmodern and post-structural ideas about how language and representation function and characterize our human experiences of this world.
>
> (Holland, 2013: 8)

This work of salvaging the past is not nostalgic or merely reconstructive, but an effort to explore what Mark Fisher called "spectres of lost futures." What haunts these texts is not (or not only) what no longer exists, but what never materialized in the first place (Fisher, 2014: 19–27). Such tendencies in contemporary rethinking of the historical novel can be seen in the backwards or anti-chronological narration of history in Yehoshua's *Mr. Mani*, in Jenny Erpenbeck's different and successive versions of history in *The End of Days*, and in history's spectral presence in Deborah Levy's *The Man Who Saw Everything*, where *both* the past *and* the future haunt the present. Such recent examples of historiographic metafiction highlight the failures of the historical record, represent multiple viewpoints and alternative histories, and foreground the enunciative situations in which the past is reproduced and narrated, read, and debated. They disrupt realist and linear reconstructions of history and question causality in their return to the past: the Holocaust, the Spanish Civil War, the dissolution of the Soviet Block, or the formation of the state of Israel, in order to examine junctions at which past opportunities were missed, and to revive futures that never happened.

5

AUTOFICTION
TROUBLING AUTOBIOGRAPHICAL ASSUMPTIONS

As in the case of historiographic metafiction, questions of referentiality and generic distinctions permeate both the definition and discussion of autofiction, a term first coined by Serge Doubrovsky to describe his 1977 novel *Fils*. The use of the word "autofiction" arose in the context of critical writing about autobiography, particularly by Philippe Lejeune in his influential discussion of the genre in *The Autobiographical Pact*. First published in France in 1975, this work defines autobiography as a "retrospective prose narrative written by a real person concerning his own existence, where the focus is his individual life, in particular the story of his personality" (Lejeune, 1989: 4). In such a text, Lejeune argued, there is an implicit referential pact between the author and the reader that "the *author*, the *narrator*, and the *protagonist* must be identical" (Lejeune, 1989: 5). Autobiography is understood, in other words, as a contractual genre that guarantees identity between author and narrator as well as between that narrator and the protagonist depicted in the text. An autobiography thus differs from an autobiographical novel, explains Lejeune, the latter being a fictional text in which similarities

DOI: 10.4324/9781003180951-6

between author and protagonist exist and may be detected by the reader, yet are not confirmed by the author (Lejeune, 1989: 13). In his efforts to distinguish autobiography from fiction and to assert the autobiographical narrative's referential status, Lejeune relies crucially on the reader's role and on a contractual relationship between that reader and the author. In a sense, autobiography results from the production of a reader who consents to read the text autobiographically, who agrees to the autobiographical pact (Boyle, 2007: 14). His definition must also rely on paratextual support of the autobiographical pact and on the world outside the text for confirmation of its generic status as autobiography, as "neither the autobiographical pact nor its concomitant referential pact can be concluded (or analyzed) by taking into consideration the text alone" (Kacandes, 2012: 381).

Doubrovsky's *Fils* directly disturbed Lejeune's claims about autobiography on the book's back cover, where he argued for his text's blending of fact and fiction, and asserted his own irreverent take on the genre:

> Autobiography? No, that's a privilege reserved for important people of this world, at the end of their lives, written in an elegant style. Fiction, then, of events and facts that are strictly real. Call it autofiction, if you will, for having entrusted the language of an adventure to the adventure of language, beyond any wisdom or syntax of the novel, whether traditional or new.
>
> (Doubrovsky, 1977; Gratton, 2001: 87, translation revised)

Doubrovsky signals here a contestation of generic definitions and distinctions between fact and fiction, but he also challenges the social order by asserting the right of anyone to write an autobiographical text. He aligns himself with experimental writing that conceives of language itself as "an adventure," and signals his kinship with new approaches to autobiographical writing in France, seen already in such texts as Georges Perec's *W, or the Memory of Childhood* (1975) and *Roland Barthes by Roland Barthes* (1975). As Philippe Gasparini has noted, Doubrovsky's statement is both political and critical, made at a time when the value of such works was tied to their revolutionary potential, and facilitated by the fact that Doubrovsky was both a writer and a critic himself (Gasparini, 2016: 177–178). His intervention was thus both creative and critical, both autobiographical text and autobiographical commentary.

DEFINING AUTOFICTION

Characterized as a challenge to previous definitions of auto-biography, autofiction is a kind of autobiographical writing that poses both epistemological questions about the nature of the subject and subjectivity, and generic questions about auto-biography. It has been defined as pertaining to texts "that are both fictional and autobiographical, and that focus on the inevitable cleavage between the subject (the Self), the protagonist, and the narrative voice" (Heidenreich 2018: 12), and seen to designate "a wide range of literary texts addressing the question of where the boundary lies between novels and autobiographies, between fictionality and factuality" (Gronemann, 2019: 241). Whether conceived as a new genre or a new mode of autobiographical writing, autofiction's rise and importance in both creative and critical writings reveals it to be "highly attuned with an age in which the subject is no longer accepted to be a unified, simple whole" (Jones, 2009: 177) and expressive of the contemporary period in which "concepts of truth, sincerity, subjectivity, publicity and privacy are in doubt" (Nicol, 2018: 272). But autofiction's popularity in recent decades has also led to critical reaction against this upstart genre or "portmanteau term" (Nicol, 2018: 255). Critics like Gérard Genette and Philippe Lejeune continue to view autofiction as inherently contradictory ("It is I and it is not I," writes Genette of its premise) (Genette, 1993: 77). They have responded with attempts to further patrol the boundary between fiction and autobiography (see especially Genette, 1993: 73–75 and Lejeune, 1987: 25–26, 37–72) or to further categorize, differentiate, and create new typologies for autofictional texts depending on the degree of their referentiality and the extent to which their narrative techniques partake more of fictional or of autobiographical writing (see Lecarme and Lecarme-Tabone, 1999: 269–271; Colonna, 2004: 199; Gasparini, 2016: 209). In his study of American autobiography, Timothy Adams notes different names for autofiction itself, including faction, non-fictional novels, autobiographical novels, factual fictions, and fictional autobiographies (Adams, 1990: 6).

Other critics have welcomed autofiction's transformation and renewal of classic autobiographical writing and theory alike. They see autofiction as responsible for opening up a new field that rivals the novel, that offers a new space for self-theorization, and that has been particularly valuable for feminist writing (see Lecarme 1993; Darrieussecq 1996; Gasparini 2004, 2016; Er 2018; Lévesque-Jalbert 2020). Since Doubrovsky's *Fils*, autofiction has moved beyond its place of origin in French letters to become a wide-ranging and diverse practice. Critics have continued to attend to its generic hybridity and to its implicit critique of autobiography (Darrieussecq, 2007; Er, 2018). They have also focused on its self-reflexivity and affiliation with metafictional and postmodernist techniques (Nicol, 2018); on the self-consciously constructed nature of its truth (Lévesque-Jalbert, 2020); on its historical roots in a period that saw myriad contestations of our ability to access "definitive truths about the past or the self" (Gratton, 2001: 86); and on its deconstruction of the genre of autobiography itself in light of poststructuralist understanding of the subject as a product of systems that the subject cannot fully master (Boyle, 2007). They see autofiction as a modern twist on the reappearance of the author after his presumed death, this last observation by the author of "The Death of the Author" himself (Barthes qtd. in Gasparini, 2016: 189), and as a transhistorical term that can be used retrospectively to describe works by Dante, Proust, Joyce, and other, earlier, would-be practitioners of autofiction (Darrieussecq, 2007; Gasparini, 2016: 209–210).

Much of the characterization of this new form of writing has attempted to describe very diverse writing practices used by autofictional texts, ones that differ significantly from each other in their modes of representation and in the degree to which they affirm or trouble the identity between author, narrator, and protagonist. Autofictional texts thus include works where the protagonist or one of the characters bears the same name as the author on the title page, as in *Everything Is Illuminated* and *Soldiers of*

Salamis discussed in the previous chapter, as well as Bruce Chatwin's *The Songlines*, Philip Roth's *Deception*, J. M. Coetzee's *Boyhood* and *Youth*, Sheila Heti's *How Should a Person Be?*, Karl Ove Knausgaard's *My Struggle*, and Dag Solstad's "Telemark novel," whose factual plot "consists for the most part of detailed accounts of the birth, marriages, deaths, and property transactions of Solstad's ancestors in Telemark from 1591 to 1896" (Davis, 2021: 417). Since the genre has been influential in comics as well as prose narratives, a pictorial representation of the author might also be taken as indication of the author's identity with the protagonist or a character in the text, as seen in Lynda Barry's *One! Hundred! Demons!* or Alison Bechdel's *Fun Home*. But autofiction also includes works where a definite similarity can be discerned between the author and the protagonist-narrator, or one of the main characters, even if the author is unnamed or bears a different name from the author. Such autofictional writing calls homonymity into question and admits other means, "besides nouns and pronouns," of identifying the hero with the author. These, Gasparini suggests, might include "their age, socio-cultural milieu, profession, aspirations," elements used by the author to play on the disjunction between author and narrator-character (Gasparini, 2004: 25). Such works include Hervé Guibert's *My Parents*, Teju Cole's *Every Day Is for the Thief* and *Open City*, W. G. Sebald's *The Emigrants*, Jenny Offill's *Dept. of Speculation*, Sherman Alexie's *The Absolutely True Diary of a Part-Time Indian*, Ben Lerner's *Leaving the Atocha Station*, and Rachel Cusk's *Outline Trilogy*.

As implied in Lejeune's definition of autobiography, paratextual elements within the text and written by its author (what Genette calls "autographic peritexts") or by someone else (what Genette calls "allographic peritexts"), or external to the text proper (e.g. publishers' classifications on the front or back cover, promotional material about the book, prefatory texts by the author in the text, etc.) play an important and interesting role in autofiction also. But, in the case of this hybrid genre, such elements often work, like the fictional editor's notes in the work of Borges, to question and reflect on the text's referential status or to further destabilize the reader's expectations or grasp of generic boundaries. The cover of Sheila Heti's *How Should a Person Be?*, for example, immediately signals its hybridity by describing the text as "a novel from life" (Heti, 2012); Guibert's *My Parents* indicates the narrator's birthday as one that corresponds to that of the book's author and, toward the end of the narrative has the father explaining why he named the narrator "Hervé." Yet the narrator also refers to a *novel* he is writing titled *My Parents*, and the back cover of the English paperback edition refers to the text as a "captivating mix" of autobiography and fiction. Another interesting and playful instance of generic frame-breaking is Dave Eggers's extensive autofictive autographic peritexts in *A Heartbreaking Work of Staggering Genius* (2001) that explore a variety of issues, including the process of writing autobiographical texts itself: from his note on the copyright page, to prefaces, acknowledgements, a guide to the text's use of symbols and metaphors, and an appendix that contains yet more self-conscious discussion of the work. These also explicitly and playfully address the work's mix of fiction and non-fiction (see Nicol, 2018: 268–270). The book's "Preface to This Edition" begins by saying that "For all the author's bluster elsewhere, this is not, actually, a work of pure nonfiction. Many parts have been fictionalized in varying degrees, for various purposes" (Eggers, 2001: ix), whereas the note on the copyright page tells us that:

> This is a work of fiction, only in that in many cases, the author could not remember the exact words said by certain people, and exact descriptions of certain things, so had to fill in gaps as best he could. Otherwise, all characters and incidents and dialogue are real, are not products of the author's imagination, because at the time of this writing, the author had no imagination whatsoever for those sorts of things, and could not conceive of *making up* a story of characters—it felt like driving a car in a clown suit—especially when there was so much to say about his own, true, sorry and inspirational story, the actual people that he has known, and of course the many twists and turns of his own thrilling and complex mind. Any resemblance to persons living or dead should be plainly apparent to them and those who know them, especially if the author has been kind enough to have provided their real names and, in some cases, their phone

numbers. All events described herein actually happened, though on occasion the author has taken certain, very small, liberties with chronology, because that is his right as an American.

(Eggers, 2001)

Eggers's frame-breaking commentaries on his text are offered as explanatory or critical assessments of it, but work most forcefully to destabilize both a reading of the text as purely fictional or as purely autobiographical. That is their point.

With these metafictional techniques, Eggers discusses problems of genre, of reading, and of interpretation, all of which make up part of the very text we are reading. His is a good example of why auto-fiction is metafictional: it both "systematically and self-consciously" (to use Patricia Waugh's definition of metafiction) blurs the lines between fiction and non-fiction, and also shows that the autofic-tional text combines autobiographical elements with auto-biographical criticism and theory. Like metafiction, autofiction is what Mark Currie would call a "borderline discourse" (Currie, 1995: 2), a type of writing that plays with the borderline between fiction and criticism. And just as historiographic metafiction asks pointed questions about the nature of historical knowledge and the problem of historical truth, so autofiction, a discourse centred on the subject and on the nature of subjectivity, is also an inquiry into the nature of the self, and our ability to know and to represent that self in language or narrative. It is a generic hybrid that arose not only out of theorizations of autobiography in 1970s France, but also, like historiographic metafiction, came into being during a period animated by poststructuralist discussions about truth, iden-tity, authority, and language. Such poststructuralist theorizations saw the subject as an entity produced, shaped, and constrained by various systems: by the Symbolic order for Jacques Lacan, by lan-guage for Roland Barthes, by discourse for Michel Foucault, by ideology for Louis Althusser (see Boyle, 2007: 22–26), and thus not in a position of mastery even over its own representation in auto-biographical narratives. They also questioned the assumption that, as Paul de Man succinctly put it, "life *produces* the autobiography as an act produces its consequences." "[C]an we not suggest, with equal justice," he asks, "that the autobiographical project may itself produce and determine the life and that whatever the writer *does* is in fact governed by the technical demands of self-portraiture and thus determined, in all its aspects, by the resources of its medium?" (De Man, 1984: 69).

Arising from this historical context and from this questioning of generic assumptions, autofiction opens up further spaces for theorizing about autobiographical narratives within autobiographical narratives. The following discussion will explore several such texts to see what aspects of the self and of the genre of autobiography they scrutinize. It will begin by examining texts that directly challenge the boundary between fiction and non-fiction and question the referential assumptions of autobiography, as seen in Roland Barthes's *Roland Barthes by Roland Barthes* and Alison Bechdel's *Fun Home*; then explore works that use autofiction to explore the nature of subjectivity and the difficulty of knowing or representing the subject in autobiographical writing, as seen in Rachel Cusk's *Outline* and Karl Ove Knausgaard's *My Struggle*. Finally, this chapter will examine recent experiments in self-writing by Carmen Maria Machado (*In the Dream House*) and Deborah Levy (her "living autobiographies") in order to explore how autotheoretical texts like theirs blend autobiography and theory to deepen not only our understanding of the subject, but also our understanding of gender.

ROLAND BARTHES AND ALISON BECHDEL: QUESTIONING THE AUTOBIOGRAPHICAL PROJECT

Soon after its publication, *Roland Barthes by Roland Barthes* was dubbed an anti-biography for fundamentally questioning any presumed equivalence between the autobiographical subject in the text and the living author who wrote it (Brée, 1978: 9). In France, this work also represented an intervention in Le Seuil's *Ecrivains de toujours* (*Writers for the Ages*) series, for which Barthes had previously written a volume on Michelet. The subtitle and rubric of this series is *"par lui-même"* (by himself) and the eclectic format of the volumes typically includes various kinds of texts—author photographs or reproductions of portraits, facsimiles of manuscript pages, italicized quotations from the author's work or letters, often in the first person, and plain type narrative passages about the author in the third person. Because the volumes of this publication series are composed of canonical authors long dead, and almost all male, the author of each volume is necessarily other than its subject despite the book's subtitle. Barthes's 1975 volume was unusual not only in being a text about a living author, but also in being the only one composed literally "*par lui-même,*" by the author himself. He used the occasion to question both the assumptions of autobiography as a genre and, more pointedly, its referential status in making an equivalence between author and narrator-character. In the text, Barthes shifts continuously between the pronominal subjects "I," "he" and "R.B." and in this way destabilizes both reference and meaning (see Allen, 2003: 106). And while autobiography is directly signalled by the book's very title, Barthes has classified the work in an interview as "a novel" and "as novelistic" (Barthes, 1985: 223). In both form and content, *Roland Barthes by Roland Barthes* insists that autobiography is not supported by a structure of reference. To begin, the text is rendered in a series of fragments that explore different topics. This piecemeal elaboration not only undermines narrative cohesion, but also upends the kind of sustained and chronological narrative of the subject and the development of his personality that is a key element of Lejeune's characterization of the genre. Additionally, that these fragments are organized according to the arbitrary order of the alphabet serves to highlight language and its structuration of experience, thus again undermining any sequential internal logic tied to the autobiographical subject's development.

Of the many sections that undertake discussion of the subject and of the nature of subjectivity, the section titled "Coincidence" is one of the most important in its reassessment of the referential assumptions of autobiographical narratives. The very word "coincidence" is a play with meaning in this section that both explores the ways in which the author coincides with the content of the autobiographical text, and the ways in which any such correspondence is just happenstance and has no inherent, causal connection. This section opens with scenarios describing Barthes listening to himself play the piano or writing on what he has already written, both specular projects that, like autobiography, involve self-analysis and self-discussion. Here Barthes disavows the possibility of coincidence or autobiographical truth, creating a pact with his reader that forbids such equivalences:

> I do not strive to put my present expression in the service of my previous truth (in the classical system, such an effort would have been sanctified under the name of *authenticity*), I abandon the exhausting pursuit of an old piece of myself, I do not try to *restore* myself (as we say of a monument). I do not say: "I am going to describe myself" but: "I am writing a text, and I call it R. B." I shift from imitation (from description) and entrust myself to nomination. Do I not know that, *in the field of the subject, there is no referent?*

(Barthes, 1977c: 56)

In this anti-autobiographical pact, the shift is to the text and to linguistic acts of nomination, with the understanding that these are not identical with the self who is writing about himself. In Barthes's scenarios, the distance between the self and the self-observing self is highlighted to reveal the chasm between those two positions and the impossibility of the subject's "present expression" aligning with his "previous truth." Language may promote the illusion of correspondence between these two entities, but, because language is a self-contained signifying system, such coincidence with what lies outside the text, and indeed, outside the system of language, cannot occur. The autobiographical project (*"[w]riting myself"*) is, writes Barthes, more aptly described as a process where one becomes one's own symbol, where one is "freewheeling in language" (Barthes, 1977c: 56). The autobiographical subject is thereby also "merely an effect of language" (Barthes, 1977c: 56, 79). What animates Barthes's desire to break the referential pact, in other words, is the same desire he expressed earlier in "The Death of the Author," namely that plural, freewheeling meaning can only occur where the text is liberated from its reference, which, in autobiography, is also its author. Accordingly, the idea of a kind of writing about the self that would end such free play, can only be understood as "suicide" (Barthes, 1977c: 56).

Yet Barthes's text, despite inveighing against autobiography's assumptions, tauntingly also provides what we might call referential traces of the subject in the text. The epigraph to his volume, an injunction to read his autobiographical text as a fiction, reads: "It must all be considered as if spoken by a character in a novel" (Barthes, 1977c). And yet, as critics have noted, the injunction is in the author's handwriting, and thereby playfully a trace of that subject or referent, his individual mark in language (Eakin, 1992: 23; Boyle, 2007: 24). This initial trace of the author is supplemented at the end of the book by two others that, respectively, problematize signification and deny any endpoint to the subject's desire, that is, to the ability to fully capture the subject in the text. The first of these is composed of doodles, described as instances where "the signifier has no signified"; the second is titled "And after?" reminding us that the process of writing the self of autobiography is never done, never complete (Barthes, 1977c: 187–188). Similarly, Barthes's "image-repertoire," comprising the many photographs of the author and of the author's family at different points in his life, these a staple of the "Ecrivains de toujours" format, tempts the reader to think in terms of a referent to the self that is inscribed in the text while this very operation is insistently disavowed by the textual fragments.

As in Barthes's text, we might well read Alison Bechdel's comic autobiography, *Fun Home*, as locating itself at the constructivist end of the spectrum, along a continuum extending from autobiography as a referential practice to autobiography as a practice through which the self is textually constructed, ultimately fictional. After all, Bechdel insists in this comic autobiography about her family, her father's suicide, and her own emerging lesbian identity that her parents are most real to [her] in fictional terms" (Bechdel, 2007: 67), thus reversing the conventional understanding of fact and fiction. Her constant allusions to and intertextual engagement with texts like *Ulysses, Portrait of the Artist as a Young Man, A Happy Death, The Myth of Sisyphus,* and *The Great Gatsby,* among many others, as analogues of her family's tragicomedy, move us to experience her narrative in textual, even fictional, terms, inseparable and indistinguishable from modes of storytelling. Thus the most intimate conversation between Alison and her father is dubbed their "Ithaca moment" (Bechdel, 2007: 222), and various other intertextual references, from an image of Tolstoy's *Anna Karenina* lying on the living room rug to signal the conundrums of unhappy families to a CD of Pergolesi's *Stabat Mater* to indicate her mother's troubled response to Bechdel's coming out letter (Bechdel, 2007: 3, 77), appear throughout the text as means of reminding us how these issues have been thematized already, by others elsewhere.

Like *Roland Barthes by Roland Barthes, Fun Home* is specular, providing instances of mirroring that reveal "that gaping rift between signifier and signified" (Bechdel, 2007: 143). One might turn especially to chapter five of Bechdel's text, which depicts Alison's early autobiographical writing and the uncertainty that creeps into her diary, creating doubt about even the most ordinary and substantial of her narrative assertions there: "It was a sort of epistemological crisis. How did I know that the things I was writing were absolutely, objectively true? My simple, declarative sentences began to strike me as hubristic at best, utter lies at worst" (Bechdel, 2007: 141). The young Alison resolves this uncertainty by inserting "the minutely-lettered phrase *I think* ... between [her] comments" in the diary (Bechdel, 2007: 141). The crisis worsens, however, with Alison creating a curvy circumflex as "a shorthand version of *I think*," then realizing she "could draw the symbol over an entire entry" (Bechdel, 2007: 142–143). It is only retrospectively that the older autobiographical narrator characterizes this form of doubt as an epistemological crisis. This observation, however, might well be taken to extend to *Fun Home* as a whole, itself marked by the same lingering question of the adequacy or coincidence of writing to reality. As such, the epistemological crisis displayed in the diary entries doubles for that of *Fun Home* itself, where its tight organizational schema, signalled by the literary thematics of each chapter, serves as a means of keeping "life's attendant chaos" (Bechdel, 2007: 149) at bay and thus making sense of disparate experience. Chapter five's image of Alison reading Dr Spock is an additional nod to the way we can read this chapter as a *mise en abyme* of the narrative as a whole and as another instance of reflection on the autobiographical project. Alison's reading of Dr Spock, described as "a curious experience in which I was both subject and object" (Bechdel, 2007: 138), is after all a succinct summary of the autobiographical enterprise itself. In this early meta-autobiographical moment, Dr Spock may seem right on the mark in accurately describing her experience. But the relationship of the older Alison to textuality is more complex and more questioning in nature.

In one sense, then, *Fun Home*'s vacillation between creating and questioning, structuring and unravelling, effectively addresses the challenges inherent in autobiographical writing. Its intertextual web means that we are forever lodged in a textual realm where books and selves merge to occupy a single, spatial field, wherein we must own up to that rift between signifier and signified, between chaos and order. *Fun Home* highlights literature's structuration of life by creating a tight schema or a series of funhouses within which lived experience often becomes subsumed in a *mise en abyme*, a symbolic chain. We can then say that when Alison writes "my parents are most real to me in fictional terms" (Bechdel, 2007: 67) we have reached a Barthesian moment of the self as the effect of language. Whether using alphabetized fragments or comics panels that overlay different temporal moments, Barthes and Bechdel's texts undercut both causality and progression in the elaboration of the self in self-reflexive autobiographies that also problematize the distinction between life and art, self and text. Like John Barth's story about referentiality, "Ambrose His Mark," *Roland Barthes by Roland Barthes* and *Fun Home* explore the philosophical conundrums that trouble the autobiographical enterprise, reminding us that selves and texts are "neither one nor quite two" (Barth, 1988a: 34).

RETHINKING THE NOVEL: THE AUTOFICTIONS OF RACHEL CUSK AND KARL OVE KNAUSGAARD

Like Karl Ove Knausgaard, who famously expressed misgivings about the novel in the second of his six-volume autofiction, *My Struggle*, saying that "just the thought of fiction, just the thought of a fabricated character in a fabricated plot made me feel nauseous" (Knausgaard, 2014: 568), Rachel Cusk has also questioned the value of fiction in the leadup to the publication of her novel *Outline*. This novel followed the publications of Cusk's three memoirs: *A Life's Work: On Becoming a Mother* (2001), *The Last Supper: A Summer in Italy* (2009), and *Aftermath*

(2012), about the breakdown of her marriage, when she struggled both to write and to read, and found novels particularly pointless: they felt

> fake and embarrassing ... the idea of making up John and Jane and having them do things together seems utterly ridiculous: Yet my mode of autobiography had come to an end. I could not do it without being misunderstood and making people angry.
>
> (Kellaway, 2014)

Outline comes out of such misgivings about both fiction and autobiography, and is part of a new mode of writing for Cusk that blends the two. It continues in the vein of the auto-biographical texts in its concern about life in the aftermath of divorce, and it focuses on the life experiences of a writer; but it distances itself from Cusk's own life in belatedly naming the protagonist Faye and in making Faye's characteristics somewhat different from her own. Like Barthes's autofiction, hers simultaneously gestures toward the real yet remains "novelistic." Such works as Cusk's and Knausgaard's follow in the footsteps of W. G. Sebald's ground-breaking experimentation with the novel form in works like *The Emigrants* (1992) and *Austerlitz* (2001) that hover mid-genre and read as autobiographical or biographical ruminations, replete with his signature documentary-like photographs, while also eschewing reference. While Cusk traces the kind of writing she arrived at in *Outline* to the vitriol that followed the publication of her non-fiction and to her sense of the novel's artificiality, her work is clearly indebted to a rethinking about the novel in recent decades, and more particularly to autofictional works like Sebald's and Knausgaard's that opened up a new way to write about the self and others.

As mentioned, *Outline*'s narrator-protagonist is named Faye, not Rachel. But the book is about a recently divorced female writer with two children who travels to Athens, Greece to teach a writing workshop, details that clearly correspond to Rachel Cusk's own life. Rather than being a book about this writer-narrator, however, *Outline* tends to make her invisible, largely a recipient of the narratives told to her by the people she meets. It is a novel that one could clearly call metafictional given the centrality of writing and writers and also of embedded narratives in it. It is a text that is rife with both narrational and figural embedding, filled with discussions about the aporia between writing and living, between experience and representation. Central among the novel's metafictional themes is its point that our reality is "storied," made up of narratives we construct about our lives. Cusk's very suspicion of fiction, quoted above, is thus echoed in the novel's focus on the function and prominence of stories as fictional constructs, as narratives we tell ourselves about our lives that, despite their power and influence, are but subjective, incomplete, and temporary versions of reality. Such instances of storied reality fill the pages of *Outline:* Marriage is understood as "a story" shared by a couple (Cusk, 2014: 12); the man Faye meets on the plane tells her various stories about his marriages, none satisfactory; indeed, the narrator notes that she senses in one of these stories that "the truth was being sacrificed to the narrator's desire to win" (Cusk, 2014: 30); a fellow writer named Ryan tells her he no longer recognizes himself in the stories he wrote (Cusk, 2014: 45); she notes that her sons begin to fight once their shared story, their shared imaginary world, is undone (Cusk, 2014: 80–81); Paniotis, the owner of a publishing house, tells her that we are all addicted to "the story of improvement" (Cusk, 2014: 99); intense moments that are lost, says Paniotis, are lost because "there is no particular story attached to them" (Cusk, 2014: 123); stories' ability to capture life makes up both the content and the discussion of the participants in Faye's writing workshops (Cusk, 2014: 137–158 and 201–226); an editor of a publishing house says that because her "relationships have had no story" she finds herself wanting to jump ahead of herself "the way [she] used to turn the pages of a book to find out what happens in the final chapter" (Cusk, 2014: 191); and a female writer named Anne, who is the next occupant of Faye's rented apartment, tells her of her curious new tendency to sum things up—not just books, but also people—and so to dispense with narrative altogether (Cusk, 2014: 232–233). This notion about stories is hardly new, of course. But where *Outline* is innovative is in its autofictional exploration of the subject and of subjectivity, specifically its refusal to construct a narrator as the central focus of the text or, more generally, its view of subjectivity as unknowable outside the stories we tell ourselves and others about it. Not only is reality based on narrative, suggests *Outline*, but "the whole idea of a 'real' self might be illusory" (Cusk, 2014: 105).

Karl Ove Knausgaard, whose influence on Cusk is clear, remains perhaps the twenty-first century's poster boy for autofiction. His six-volume work, titled *My Struggle*, details his family life and his struggles as an individual and as an artist, themes also explored in Cusk's *Outline* trilogy. Published between 2009 and 2011, and totalling over 3,500 pages, he has been dubbed by some a modern-day Proust. But Knausgaard's writing is raw, and in it he names and discusses his relations with friends and family members that leave no ambiguity about the identity of his characters, the real-life counterparts to his fiction. Indeed, his work has had very real consequences on his relationships (Hughes, 2014; Rothman, 2018), something Knausgaard acknowledges in the work itself when he writes on the last page of the final volume: "I will never forgive myself for what I've exposed [my wife and children] to, but I did it, and I will have to live with it" (Knausgaard, 2018: 1152). These novels challenge generic boundaries with writing that would seem to abide by Lejeune's autobiographical pact but which insists on the work's fictional status. That, writes Toril Moi in her appraisal of the work's innovativeness, is precisely their point, to "break with the old conventions of reading" and with the tradition of the novel itself (Moi, 2017b).

The newness of this work, that is, is largely due to the different kinds of demands it places on its readers to find new criteria with which to understand and explore it. The novel's wiliness with respect to generic categorizations is part and parcel of its challenge to ingrained or traditional ways of reading, and its "genuine effort to figure out what it means to write a novel in a new aesthetic and historical dispensation" (Moi, 2017b). But works such as Knausgaard's and Cusk's also partake of autofiction's aim, as Marie Darrieussecq has written, to renew literary codes, particularly those of autobiography. They ask us not only to rethink the novel, but the genre of autobiography and the question of reference as well. On the one hand they try to sensitize us to the experiential minutiae that make up daily life and thus to bring us "closer to reality," but on the other hand, these texts' self-consciousness about the storied nature of lives and the "problem with all representation" (Knausgaard, 2014: 486–487) makes us aware of the impossibility of ever doing so. At heart, the impulses of such autofiction, in its questioning of the self and of the nature of subjectivity, and in its rethinking of conventional modes of self-portraiture in both fiction and autobiography, return us to the exploration of the relation between art and life, between writing and criticism, that lie at the heart of metafiction.

THE AUTOTHEORIZATIONS OF CARMEN MARIA MACHADO AND DEBORAH LEVY

Recent examples of autofiction have importantly insisted on the structural, political, and cultural dimensions of identity, taking an expansive and critical look at identity that implicitly resists the self-focus trend Cusk noted in a 2014 interview when she said that "autobiography is increasingly the only form in all the arts" (Kellaway, 2014). Carmen Maria Machado's *In the Dream House*, and Deborah Levy's trio of "living autobiographies" (*Things I Don't Want to Know, The Cost of Living*, and *Real Estate*) reframe the question of identity, elaborating a self in relation to narrative tropes and power structures in order to put the individual life in the context of broader theoretical questions and political considerations. Their work is part of an increased autotheoretical element in autobiographical writing that seeks to stage an "encounter between first-person narration and theory" (Wiegman, 2020: 1). Autotheory, a hybrid genre that is itself composed of the hybrid genre of autofiction plus critical theory, has been seen as an interesting tendency in current autobiographical writing that is at once seeking an alternative to the memoir and responding to the institutionalization of theory in the academy and beyond (see Laubender, 2020: 49–50; and Clare, 2020: 103). Often, as works by Machado and Levy exemplify, autotheory has been noted for its roots in feminist or gender theory, for constituting a feminist fourth wave with a fresh perspective on the adage "the personal is political," and for its enrichment of feminist practices (see Wiegman, 2020; Fournier, 2018, Fournier, 2021; and Lévesque-Jalbert, 2020). Not an entirely new phenomenon, but one that has its antecedents in works by such diverse twentieth-century writers as Sigmund Freud, Walter Benjamin, Julia Kristeva, Roland Barthes, Eve Sedgewick, Gloria Anzaldúa, bell hooks, Carolyn Kay Steedman, and Fred Wah (see Clare, 2020: 88–89), it has received increased attention with the 2015 publication of Maggie Nelson's *The Argonauts* whose title is derived from a passage in *Roland Barthes by Roland Barthes*. Autotheory extends the questions posed by autofictional writing and combines them with theoretical discourse in a text that makes plain its theoretical affiliations. Like many metafictional and autofictional texts, autotheoretical ones use a variety of devices: different fonts, marginal notes, self-commentary, intertextuality, epigraphs, and prologues, to produce a complex, plural text, that, like autofiction, challenges notions of the self as autonomous, cohesive or representable while simultaneously weaving this self's encounter with the discourses and structures that inform its lived experience into the very fabric of the text.

Machado's *In the Dream House*, a highly metafictional memoir that foregrounds its own structuring devices and proposes to find a means of filling in the "archival silence" on domestic abuse in queer relationships, echoes many of the structuring tropes of Roland Barthes's *A Lover's Discourse: Fragments*. Like Barthes's text on the lover, Machado's text comments on its own format, and it too is fragmented, each section offering its own organizational schema, many of which are derived from literary criticism and theory (*Dream House as* Picaresque, as Lesbian Cult Classic, as Romance Novel, as Bildungseroman, as American Gothic, or as Lipogram, to name but a few). Both texts position themselves as elaborating a discourse that is "*of an extreme solitude*" (Barthes, 1978: 1), and utilize the fragments that make up their texts as a means of undercutting narrative; "the figures are distributional but not integrative," writes Barthes, affirming what is true of Machado's narrative content also (Barthes, 1978: 7). For Barthes, the deliberate frustration of any coherent, linear narrative has to do with the very triviality that makes up the amorous life: "'I ran into X, who was with Y', 'Today X didn't call me' 'X was in a bad mood,' etc.: who would see a story in that?" (Barthes, 1978: 7, 93). And while Machado's amorous experience is also made up of trivial events, the fragmentation of *In the Dream House* has more to do with the absence of any narrative models for writing her story. Searching to fill in this absence, she can only utilize postures already in existence, forms already available. Thus each fragment is a new experiment in telling the tale, each a possible brick of the so-called *Dream House*, a possible way of narrating lived experience. The strategy works to keep *In the Dream House* open-ended, resisting any "real ending" (Machado, 2019: 239) while simultaneously conveying its content: the events, feelings, thoughts, and reflections that make up the discourse and experience of the queer subject of domestic violence. Even this subject is split in the text, made up of the victimized "you" used in the chapters detailing domestic abuse, and the "I" that retrospectively narrates the experiences of this "you" used primarily at the beginning and the end of the text. For example, in the chapter titled "*Dream House as* Choose Your Own Adventure®," the "you," rather than an "I", is used to describe the experience of waking up to face the lover's accusing look: "When you turn over, she is staring at you. The luminous innocence of the light curdles in your stomach. You don't remember ever going from awake to afraid so quickly" (Machado, 2019: 162). The "I" is used in the chapter titled "*Dream House as* Prologue," where Machado describes her project: "I enter into the archive that domestic abuse between partners who share a gender identity is both possible and not uncommon, and that it can look something like this. I speak into the silence. I toss the stone of my story into a vast crevice; measure the emptiness by its small sound" (Machado, 2019: 5). In these ways, Machado problematizes representation and self-narration. Her account's use of intertextuality and paratextuality, and of multiple, possible literary tropes and theorizations to retell her experience makes plain the many ways and kinds of texts through which autobiographical narration can thread its story.

While Deborah Levy's trilogy of "living autobiographies," *Things I Don't Want to Know* (2013), *The Cost of Living* (2018), and *Real Estate* (2021a), may not immediately seem particularly metafictional, autofictional, or autotheoretical, they are nonetheless highly attuned to all three theoretical and generic perspectives in contemporary writing. Moving continually from the particular to the general, from the material to the philosophical, and from the personal to the social, Levy insists on a certain distance between the "I" in the text and herself even as she details events in her life: her "I" is an avatar, she writes; it is "myself but not quite myself" (Levy, 2021a: 256). This "I" is also often referred to in her texts as a female character, and sometimes yet more specifically, recalling novels by Rachel Cusk or Jenny Offill, as a female character who is also a female writer. The questioned referential status of the self as well as its fictionally derived correlative in the female character echo autofiction's questioning of autobiographical assumptions and evoke metafiction's self-consciousness. And as in autotheoretical texts, hers is replete with quotations from critical theory and feminist theory, citing such authors as Adrienne Rich, Marguerite Duras, Virginia Woolf, Julia Kristeva, and Simone de Beauvoir, that guide and inform her narration, and frame her own experience with respect to broad, social and political analyses. Revealing the feminist potential of autofictional and autotheoretical writing, Levy also makes sure to attend to other women's lives than her own, extrapolating from her own experiences and from those of the many other women who appear in her living autobiographies to discern the shapes and struggles that inform women's lives. Toward the end of the first volume, she writes:

> It occurred to me that both Maria and I were on the run in the twenty-first century, just like George Sand whose name was also Amantine was on the run in the nineteenth century, and Maria whose name was also Zama was looking for somewhere to recover and rest in the twentieth. We were on the run from the lies concealed in the language of politics, from myths about our character and our purpose in life. We were on the run from our own desires too probably, whatever they were. It was best to laugh it off.
>
> The way we laugh. At our own desires. The way we mock ourselves. Before anyone else can. The way we are wired to kill. Ourselves. It doesn't bear thinking about.
>
> (Levy, 2013: 158–159)

The feminist project encapsulated here demonstrates the particular relevance of the deconstruction of the autobiographical genre for women, as its very task is to untangle their selves from societal myths and desires, even their own. In an interview with Tash Aw (Levy, with Tash Aw, 2021b), Levy has spoken about a passage from Virginia Woolf's essay "Professions for Women" that influenced her project, one in which Woolf wonders what remains after the woman writer has killed the proverbial "Angel in the House," has rid herself of that falsehood, and has only to concern herself with being herself: "Ah, but what is 'herself'?," Woolf asks, "I mean, what is a woman? I assure you, I do not know. I do not believe that you know. I do not believe that anybody can know until she has expressed herself in all the arts and professions open to human skill" (Woolf, 1942: 151). As in Machado's efforts to "speak into the silence" (Machado, 2019: 5), Levy's living autobiographies are metafictional explorations of what "woman" might mean, and an attempt to clear some space for her becoming.

Interestingly, like Machado's memoir, many of Levy's autobiographical meditations, in the third volume especially, return to the question of a home or a house and what that vision or dream holds, and withholds too, for this female character. The dream for a house, for real estate, follows the making and remaking of several actual homes in Levy's trilogy: her childhood home in South Africa, her mother's home once her parents separate, the adult home she makes with her husband prior to their separation, and the home made emptier once her daughters have left for university. It is a longing for a place that would accommodate this female character's desires, but it is also more abstractly the need to refashion that home created for the female character as daughter, wife, or mother by patriarchy. Citing Adrienne Rich in *Things I Don't Want to Know*, Levy invites her reader to consider that no woman is truly at home "in the institutions fathered by masculine consciousness" (Levy, 2013: 22). And in the subsequent two volumes, in which she details her life after the dissolution of her married home, after the death of her mother, and after her daughters' departure, she explores the possibilities now open to "a nearly sixty-year-old female character," and the question of "how to live a creative life in old age" (Levy, 2021a: 188, 124). That plot or home, or the home as a modest utopia, and the desire for it, is therefore both real and unreal, material and metaphorical:

I was also searching for a house in which I could live and work and make a world at my own pace, but even in my imagination this home was blurred, undefined, not real, or not realistic, or lacked realism. I yearned for a grand old house (I had now added an oval fireplace to its architecture) and a pomegranate tree in the garden ... The wish for this home was intense, yet I could not place it geographically, nor did I know how to achieve such a spectacular house with my precarious income. All the same, I added it to my imagined property portfolio, along with a few other imagined minor properties. The house with the pomegranate tree was my major acquisition. In this sense, I owned some unreal estate.

(Levy, 2021a: 3–4)

The Edenic home imagined here is material, and costly, but it is also an idea, an "unreal estate." Its would-be inhabitant is likewise both actual and imagined: "a sixty-year-old female character, both unwritten and constantly rewriting the script" (Levy, 2021a: 294–295). Like Machado's, this script or house is one made centrally of language, that "is always in the process of being constructed and repaired. It can fall apart and be made again" (Levy 2021a: 291), so that, finally, Levy's real estate *is* her language: "the books that [she] has written" and whose royalties she bequeaths to her daughters (Levy, 2021a: 297).

Authors like Cusk, Nelson, Heti, Offill, Machado, and Levy reveal how productive autofictional self-reflexivity and autotheory have been for exploring gender and for reflecting on the personal and political dimensions of lived experience; autofiction allows them to write of the self but to reject the logic of individuated experience in favour of an "I" large enough to signify the experience of women more generally. Not only have women had an important role in shaping autofictional writing as the work of Shirley Jordan, Yanbing Er, and Emile Léveque-Jalbert have shown, but autofiction's possibilities for self-theorization, occurring as they have under conditions of the deconstruction of the subject, have opened up a space "to think the feminist point of view" and to create an "open and politically charged mode of autofictional feminist writing" (Lévesque-Jalbert, 2020: 69, 72). In writing these "living autobiographies," texts written in "the storm of life," rather than in the calm of retrospection, Levy situates feminist autobiographical practice somewhere between the realities of female existence and the utopian possibilities open to her. The self-reflexive and self-reflective impulses we see in the various autofictional texts discussed in this chapter show them to be paradigmatic of thinking in our time: texts that explore literary tropes, genres, and generic conventions, and use these to address such broad concerns as historical and political realities and such intimate concerns as our own knowledge of ourselves and the nature of our relations with others.

Exploring both the historical and the personal dimensions of experience, Chapters 4 and 5, on historiographic metafiction and autofiction, add to what earlier chapters took as metafiction: its exploration of narrative, writing, reading, interpretation, and language. Together these discussions suggest, to slightly alter Barthes's own phrase in an essay on structuralism, that metafiction might best be thought of as "essentially an *activity*" (Barthes, 1972c: 214) or, as Linda Hutcheon refers to it, a "mimesis of *process*" (Hutcheon, 1980: 39). As a highly self-conscious activity or a process that breaks down boundaries between fiction and reality, metafiction also demands that its reader participate in the act of interpretation and reflection. Metafiction's enduring attraction and continued usefulness, as such recent novels like *Trust Exercise, Pym, How to Be Both, Soldiers of Salamis*, and *Outline* show us, lie in this ability to engage us in radically and thoroughly reassessing our understanding while remaining aware that we can only do so in a medium "for experiencing experience" (Hejinian, 2000: 3).

GLOSSARY

autobiography   (Lejeune) is a retrospective prose narrative written by a real person about their life.

autobiographical pact   (Lejeune), also referred to as the referential pact in autobiographical writing, is the tacit understanding between the author and the reader that the author, narrator, and protagonist of an autobiographical text are one and the same.

autofiction   is a type of autobiographical writing that poses epistemological and generic questions about autobiography in the autobiographical text itself, and purposely blurs the boundary between fiction and fact.

autotheory   is a hybrid genre that combines first-person narration and critical theory in an autobiographical narrative.

cognitive narratology   is a critical approach to narratives that is particularly attuned to the mental states

DOI: 10.4324/9781003180951-7

that attend the experience of narrative. It focuses on the various processes readers deploy in consuming stories, and on the ways in which stories themselves make sense of experience.

figural embedding   (Chambers) involves the incorporation into a narrative of a figure that represents art or the production and reception of narrative. That figure can be an author or a reader, for example, but can also be an inanimate object, like the statue of Flaubert in *Flaubert's Parrot* by Julian Barnes.

historiographic metafiction   (Hutcheon) is a type of postmodern fiction that weds metafiction and historiography. It questions the generic boundaries between literature and history and poses epistemological questions about the nature of historical truth.

intertextuality   is a term that refers, in a limited sense, to the presence of one text in another text (Genette). More broadly, however, it is the notion that any text is located within a complex network of signifying systems (Kristeva, Barthes) and its meaning is therefore plural.

metalepsis   is a narrative effect in which the boundaries of the world of the telling of a story and the world told by a story are overrun, as when the fictional narrator of *The French Lieutenant's Woman* by John Fowles suddenly addresses the actual reader directly in chapter 13. Marie-Laure Ryan distinguishes between a brief intermingling of levels of reality that is followed by the reassertion of boundaries between levels (rhetorical metalepsis), and an intermingling of levels that results in their interpenetration and mutual contamination (ontological metalepsis).

metanarration and metareference are terms that broaden the self-referential concepts of metafiction beyond the fiction genre to narrative more broadly, and beyond narrative to diverse media forms.

mise en abyme (Dällenbach) is a particular type of figural or narrational embedding that is characterized by its similarity with the work that contains it. It is a form of embedding whereby the element embedded constitutes a reflection or mirroring within the text. An example of *mise en abyme* is the play within the play in *Hamlet*.

modernism is a period of intensified experimentation in the arts, usually dated from the late nineteenth to the middle of the twentieth century, during which artists departed from traditional forms of art. The poet Ezra Pound's injunction to "make it new" encapsulates the artistic innovation of this period as does its self-consciousness about artistic practice.

narrational embedding (Chambers) is when there is a narrative act within a narrative act or a narrative situation within a narrative situation. An example is Molina's narration of movies he has seen to his cellmate Valentin in Manuel Puig's *Kiss of the Spider Woman*.

New Criticism is an influential formalist movement in literary criticism that was especially prominent in the United States during the middle of the twentieth century. It espouses the value of close reading and conceives of the work of art as a self-contained aesthetic object whose meaning is independent of authorial intentions, readers' responses, and historical and cultural contexts.

New Historicism is a critical movement that developed in the 1980s and involved a renewed attentiveness to the historical moment in which a work of art is created. Rather than focus on the production of historical truth or on the reconstruction of the historical record, however, new historicism proceeds with the assumption that our historical understanding is a product of textuality and interpretation.

Oulipo is a shorthand for Ouvroir de littérature potentielle, and is the name of a group founded in 1960 by Françoise Le Lionnais and Raymond Queneau that created new works of literature through the use of constrained writing techniques. They invented new forms and used old ones that had fallen into disuse with the aim of highlighting the importance of linguistic and literary playfulness and enjoyment. Their practice explored the paradoxical relationship between constraint and freedom.

paratextuality (Genette) refers to all elements that exist on the threshold of a text and mediate it for the reader. These include both items within the book proper (such as epigraphs, prefaces, notes, or afterwords) as well as items outside it (such as book reviews or critical essays).

postcritique is a recent critical tendency that is informed by literary theory and ideological criticism but that seeks to restore to scholarly and pedagogical discussion a sense of readers' own engagements with literary texts, especially emotional or immersive experiences, without construing them as naive or superficial.

postmodernism

variously defined, postmodernism has been used to describe artistic practices that upend tradition by mixing ancient and modern, traditional and popular art forms, and that use parody, intertextuality, and self-reflexivity. In philosophical terms, postmodernism represents an attitude of scepticism with respect to notions of truth, value, history, and traditional authorities generally, adopting instead a questioning and relativist stance.

poststructuralism

is a movement in the humanities and social sciences that followed structuralism and its insistence on frameworks and structures. Poststructuralist theorists like Roland Barthes, Jacques Derrida, and Michel Foucault investigated the binary oppositions underlying structuralist approaches to assert instead the indeterminacy and instability of meaning.

Reader-Response Criticism

is a school of literary criticism that focuses on audience reception. Reader-response critics examine the reader's experience and interpretation of the literary text, asking such questions as the degree to which a text can sustain as many meanings as readers, or whether some readers' interpretations are more valid than others.

realism

refers to a style of narrative prose that flourished in the nineteenth century. It sought to represent life accurately, tended to focus on the middle class or occasionally the working class rather than the aristocracy, and strove to create faithful descriptions of everyday life and ordinary human psychology and behaviours.

BIBLIOGRAPHY

Abish, Walter (1974) *Alphabetical Africa*, New York, New Directions.

Abish, Walter (1987) "Interview with Walter Abish" in *Alive and Writing: Interviews with American Authors of the 1980s*, Larry McCaffery and Sinda Gregory (eds), Urbana, University of Illinois Press.

Adams, Timothy Dow (1990) *Telling Lies in Modern American Autobiography*, Chapel Hill, University of North Carolina Press.

Ahad-Legardy, Badia (2021) *Afro-Nostalgia: Feeling Good in Contemporary Black Culture*, Urbana, University of Illinois Press.

Alber, Jan and Brian Richardson (2020). "Introduction" in *Unnatural Narratology: Extensions, Revisions, and Challenges*, Jan Alber and Brian Richardson (eds), Columbus, Ohio State University Press, 8–17.

Alexie, Sherman (2009) *The Absolutely True Diary of a Part-Time Indian*, New York, Little, Brown.

Allen, Graham (2003) *Roland Barthes*, New York, Routledge.

Allen, Graham (2011) *Intertextuality*, New York, Routledge.

Alter, Robert (1975) *Partial Magic: The Novel as a Self-Conscious Genre*, Berkeley, University of California Press.

Anderson, Amanda, Rita Felski and Toril Moi (2019) *Character: Three Inquiries in Literary Studies*, Chicago, University of Chicago Press.

Anker, Elizabeth S. (2017) "Postcritical Reading, the Lyric, and Ali Smith's *How to Be Both*", *Diacritics*, 45 (4): 16–42.

Ashbery, John (2008a) "And *Ut Pictura Poesis* Is Her Name" in *Collected Poems 1956–1987*, New York, Library of America, 519–520.

Ashbery, John (2008b) "The Instruction Manual" in *Collected Poems 1956–1987*, New York, Library of America, 5–8.

Ashbery, John (2008c) "My Erotic Double" in *Collected Poems 1956–1987*, New York, Library of America, 667.

Ashbery, John (2008d) "Paradoxes and Oxymorons" in *Collected Poems 1956–1987*, New York, Library of America, 698.

Ashbery, John (2009) "The Art of Poetry", Interview with Peter Stitt, *The Paris Review Interviews*, vol. IV, New York, Picador, 174–202.

Auerbach, Erich (1953) *Mimesis: The Representation of Reality in Western Literature*, Willard R. Trask (trans.), Princeton, Princeton University Press.

Baetens, Jan (2012) "Oulipo and Proceduralism" in *The Routledge Companion to Experimental Literature*, Joe Bray, Alison Gibbons and Brian McHale (eds), New York, Routledge, 115–127.

Barker, Pat (1991) *Regeneration*, New York, Penguin Books.

Barnes, Julian (2009) *Flaubert's Parrot*, New York, Vintage.

Barry, Lynda (2002) *One! Hundred! Demons!* Seattle, Sasquatch Books.

Barth, John (1967) "The Literature of Exhaustion", *The Atlantic*, 220 (2), August: 29–34.

Barth, John (1988a) "Ambrose His Mark" in *Lost in the Funhouse*, New York, Anchor Books, 14–34.

Barth, John (1988b) "Frame-Tale" in *Lost in the Funhouse*, New York, Anchor Books, 1–2.

Barth, John (1988c) "Lost in the Funhouse" in *Lost in the Funhouse*, New York, Anchor Books, 72–97.

Barthes, Roland (1972a) "Literature and Metalanguage" in *Critical Essays*, Richard Howard (trans.), Evanston, Northwestern University Press, 97–98.

Barthes, Roland (1972b) "What Is Criticism?" in *Critical Essays*, Richard Howard (trans.), Evanston, Northwestern University Press, 255–260.

Barthes, Roland (1972c) "The Structuralist Activity" in *Critical Essays*, Richard Howard (trans.), Evanston, Northwestern University Press, 213–220.

Barthes, Roland (1974) *S/Z*, Richard Miller (trans.), New York, Hill and Wang.

Barthes, Roland (1975) *The Pleasure of the Text*, Richard Miller (trans.), New York, Hill and Wang.

Barthes, Roland (1977a) "The Death of the Author" in *Image-Music-Text*, Stephen Heath (trans.), New York, Hill and Wang, 142–148.

Barthes, Roland (1977b) "From Work to Text" in *Image-Music-Text*, Stephen Heath (trans.), New York, Hill and Wang, 155–164.

Barthes, Roland (1977c) *Roland Barthes by Roland Barthes*, Richard Howard (trans.), Berkeley, University of California Press.

Barthes, Roland (1978) *A Lover's Discourse: Fragments*, Richard Howard (trans.), New York, Hill and Wang.

Barthes, Roland (1985) *The Grain of the Voice: Interviews 1962–1980*, Linda Coverdale (trans.), New York, Hill and Wang.

Barthes, Roland (1986) *The Rustle of Language*, Richard Howard (trans.), New York, Hill and Wang.

Barthes, Roland (1989) "The Discourse of History" in *The Rustle of Language*, Richard Howard (trans.), New York, Hill and Wang, 129–140.

Bechdel, Alison (2007) *Fun Home*, New York, Mariner.

Becker, Daniel Levin (2012) *Many Subtle Channels: In Praise of Potential Literature*, Cambridge, Harvard University Press.

Bénabou, Marcel (1986) "Rule and Constraint" in *Oulipo: A Primer of Potential Literature*, Warren Motte (ed. and trans.), London, Dalkey Archive Press, 40–47.

Bök, Christian (2005) "A Few Thoughts on Beautiful Things" in *Biting the Error: Writers Explore Narrative*, Mary Burger, Robert Glück, Camille Roy, and Gail Scott (eds), Toronto, Coach House Press, 2005.

Bök, Christian (2007) "The Xenotext Experiment: An Interview with Christian Bök", *Postmodern Culture*, 17 (2) http://pmc.iath.virginia.edu/issue.107/17.2voyce.html, accessed 11 December 2021.

Bök, Christian (2009) *Eunoia*, Toronto, Coach House Press.

Borges, Jorge Luis (1964a) "The Circular Ruins" in *Labyrinths: Selected Stories & Other Writings*, New York, New Directions, 45–50.

Borges, Jorge Luis (1964b) "The Garden of Forking Paths" in *Labyrinths: Selected Stories & Other Writings*, Donald A. Yates (trans.), New York, New Directions, 19–29.

Borges, Jorge Luis (1964c) "Pierre Menard, Author of the *Quixote*" in *Selected Stories & Other Writings*, New York, New Directions, 36–44.

Borges, Jorge Luis (1997) "El jardín de senderos que se bifurcan" *in Ficciones*, Madrid, Alianza Editorial.

Borges, Jorge Luis (1998) "A Dialog about a Dialog" in *Collected Fictions*, Andrew Hurley (trans.), New York, Penguin, 295.

Boyle, Claire (2007) *Consuming Autobiographies: Reading and Writing the Self in Post-War France*, London, LEGENDA.

Brée, Germaine (1978) *Narcissus absconditus: the Problematic Art of Autobiography in Contemporary France*, Oxford, Clarendon Press.

Bucak, Ayşe Papatya (2019) "Iconography" in *The Trojan War Museum and Other Stories*, New York, Norton, 36–50.

Byatt, A. S. (2018) *Possession: A Romance*, New York, Vintage.

Calvino, Italo (1981) *If on a Winter Night a Traveler*, William Weaver (trans.), New York, Harcourt Brace.

Cercas, Javier (2000) *Relatos reales*, Barcelona, Acantilado.

Cercas, Javier (2001) *Soldados de Salamina*, Domingo Ródenas de Moya (ed.), Madrid, Cátedra.

Cercas, Javier (2017) *The Imposter*, Frank Wynne (trans.), New York, Vintage.

Cercas, Javier (2020a) *Soldiers of Salamis*, Anne McLean (trans.), New York, Vintage.

Cercas, Javier (2020b) *Lord of All the Dead: A Nonfiction Novel*, Anne McLean (trans.), New York, Vintage.

Chambers, Ross (1984) *Story and Situation: Narrative Seduction and the Power of Fiction*, Minneapolis, University of Minnesota Press.

Chambers, Ross (1991) *Room for Maneuver: Reading (the) Oppositional (in) Narrative*, Chicago, University of Chicago Press.

Chambers, Ross (1999) *Loiterature*, Lincoln, Nebraska University Press.

Choi, Susan (2019) *Trust Exercise*, New York, Henry Holt.

Clare, Ralph (2020) "Becoming Autotheory", *Arizona Quarterly*, 76 (1): 85–107.

Cohn, Dorrit (1999) *The Distinction of Fiction*, Baltimore, Johns Hopkins University Press.

Cole, Teju (2012) *Open City*, New York, Random House.

Cole, Teju (2015) *Every Day Is for the Thief*, New York, Random House.

Colonna, Vincent (2004) *Autofiction et autres mythomanies littéraires*, Auch, Tristram.

Cortázar, Julio (1966) *Hopscotch*, Gregory Rabassa (trans.) New York, Pantheon Books.

Cortázar, Julio (1967a) "Axolotl" in *Blow-Up and Other Stories*, Paul Blackburn (trans.), New York, Pantheon Books, 3–9.

Cortázar, Julio (1967b) "Continuity of Parks" in *Blow-Up and Other Stories*, Paul Blackburn (trans.), New York, Pantheon Books, 63–65.

Cortázar, Julio (1967c) "The Night Face Up" in *Blow-Up and Other Stories*, Paul Blackburn (trans.), New York, Pantheon Books, 66–76.

Cortázar, Julio and Carol Dunlop (2007) *Autonauts of the Cosmoroute*, Anne McLean (trans.), Brooklyn, NY, Archipelago Books.

Costello, Bonnie (1982) "John Ashbery and the Idea of the Reader", *Contemporary Literature*, 23 (4): 493–514.

Cowart, David (1993) *Literary Symbiosis: The Reconfigured Text in Twentieth-Century Writing*, Athens, University of Georgia Press.

Culler, Jonathan (1975) *Structuralist Poetics: Structuralism, Linguistics, and the Study of Literature*, Ithaca, Cornell University Press.

Currie, Mark (1995) "Introduction" in *Metafiction*, Mark Currie (ed.), New York, Longman, 1–18.

Cusk, Rachel (2014) *Outline*, New York, Harper Perennial.

Dällenbach, Lucien (1989) *The Mirror in the Text*, Jeremy Whiteley with Emma Hughes (trans.), Oxford, Polity Press.

Darrieussecq, Marie (1996) "L'Autofiction, un genre pas sérieux", *Poétique*, septembre 1996: 369–379.

Darrieussecq, Marie (2007) *"Je est unE autre"*. https://mariedarrieussecq.com/sites/default/files/2018-01/conférence%20donnée%20à%20Rome%20à%20un%20colloque%20sur%20l'autofiction.pdf, accessed 1 November 2021.

Davis, Kimberly Chabot (2017) "The Follies of Racial Tribalism: Mat Johnson and Anti-Utopian Satire", *Contemporary Literature* 58 (1): 18–52.

Davis, Lydia (2007a) "Example of the Continuing Past Tense in a Hotel Room" in *Varieties of Disturbance*, New York, Farrar, Straus and Giroux, 201.

Davis, Lydia (2007b) "Grammar Questions" in *Varieties of Disturbance*, New York, Farrar, Straus and Giroux, 27–29.

Davis, Lydia (2014) "Notes During Long Phone Conversation with Mother" in *Can't and Won't*, New York, Farrar, Straus and Giroux, 101.

Davis, Lydia (2019) *Essays One*, New York, Farrar, Straus and Giroux.

Davis, Lydia (2021) *Essays Two*, New York, Farrar, Straus and Giroux.

Davis, Philip (2020) *Reading for Life*, Oxford, Oxford University Press.

De Certeau, Michel (1984) *The Practice of Everyday Life*, Steve Rendall (trans.), Berkeley, University of California Press.

De Groot, Jerome (2010) *The Historical Novel*, New York, Routledge.

De Man, Paul (1984) "Autobiography as De-Facement" in *The Rhetoric of Romanticism*, New York, Columbia University Press, 67–81.

Derrida, Jacques (1978) "Structure, Sign, and Play in the Discourse of the Human Sciences" in *Writing and Difference*, Alan Bass (trans.), London, Routledge, 278–294.

Dix, Hywel (2018) "Introduction" in *Autofiction in English*, Hywel Dix (ed.), Poole, UK, Palgrave, 1–23.

Doherty, Maggie (2020) "Metafiction and #MeToo: A New Way to Write Trauma" in *The Yale Review* 108 (1), https://yalereview.yale.edu/metafiction-and-metoo, accessed 13 December 2021.

Doležel, Lubomír (2010) *Possible Worlds of Fiction and History*, Baltimore, Johns Hopkins University Press.

Doubrovsky, Serge (1977) *Fils*, Paris, Galilée.

Doubrovsky, Serge (1989) *Le Livre brisé*, Paris, Grasset.

Doubrovsky, Serge (1997) "Autofiction and Beyond": Interview with Roger Célestin, *Sites* 1 (2): 397–405.

Dyer, Geoff (2009) *Jeff in Venice, Death in Varanasi*, New York, Canongate.

Eakin, Paul John (1992) *Touching the World: Reference in Autobiography*, Princeton, Princeton University Press.

Eggers, Dave (2001) *A Heartbreaking Work of Staggering Genius*, New York, Vintage.

Elias, Amy J. (2001) *Sublime Desire: History and Post 1960s Fiction*, Baltimore, Johns Hopkins University Press.

Elias, Amy J. (2016) "Historiographic Metafiction" in *The Cambridge History of Postmodern Literature*, Brian McHale and Len Platt (eds), Cambridge, Cambridge University Press, 293–307.

Er, Yanbing (2018) "Contemporary Women's Autofiction as Critique of Postfeminist Discourse", *Australian Feminist Studies*, 33 (97): 316–330.

Erpenbeck, Jenny (2012) *The End of Days*, Susan Bernofsky (trans.), New York, New Directions.

Eugenides, Jeffrey (2011) *The Marriage Plot*, New York, Knopf.

Felski, Rita (2017) "Postcritical Reading", *American Book Review*, 38 (5): 4–5.

Ferreira-Meyers, Karen (2018) "Does Autofiction Belong to French or Francophone Authors and Readers Only?" in *Autofiction in English*, Hywel Dix (ed.), Poole, UK, Palgrave, 27–48.

Fish, Stanley (1970) "Literature in the Reader: Affective Stylistics" in *New Literary History* 2: 123–162.

Fish, Stanley (1980) *Is There a Text in This Class? The Authority of Interpretive Communities*, Cambridge, Harvard University Press.

Fish, Stanley (1997) *Surprised by Sin: The Reader in* Paradise Lost, London, Macmillan.

Fludernik, Monika (2003) "Scene, Shift, Metalepsis, and the Metaleptic Mode", *Style* 37 (4): 382–400.

Foenkinos, David (2020) *The Mystery of Henri Pick*, Sam Taylor (trans.), London, Pushkin Press.

Foer, Jonathan Safran (2002) *Everything Is Illuminated*, New York, Harper Perennial.

Foucault, Michel (1972) *The Archeology of Knowledge*, A. M. Sheridan Smith (trans.), New York, Pantheon Books.

Foucault, Michel (1977) *Discipline and Punish: The Birth of the Prison*, Alan Sheridan (trans.), New York, Pantheon Books.

Foucault, Michel (1984) "What Is an Author?" in *The Foucault Reader*, Paul Rabinow (ed.), Josué V. Harari (trans.), New York, Pantheon Books, 101–120.

Fournel, Paul et al. (2006) *The State of Constraint: New Work by Oulipo*, San Francisco, McSweeney's 22.

Fournier, Lauren (2018) "Sick Women, Sad Girls, and Selfie Theory: Autotheory as Contemporary Feminist Practice", *a/b: Auto/Biography Studies*, 33 (3): 641–660.

Fournier, Lauren (2021) *Autotheory as Feminist Practice in Art, Writing, and Criticism*, Cambridge, MIT Press.

Fowles, John (1969) *The French Lieutenant's Woman*, New York, Little, Brown and Company.

Fukuyama, Francis (1989) "The End of History?", *The National Interest*, 16: 3–18.

Fulda, Daniel (2014) "Historiographic Narration" in *The Living Handbook of Narratology*, www.lhn.uni-hamburg.de/node/123.html, accessed 11 November 2021.

Gasparini, Philippe (2004) *Est-il je? Roman autobiographique et autofiction*, Paris, Seuil.

Gasparini, Philippe (2016) *Poétique du je: du roman autobiographique à l'autofiction*, Lyon, Presses universitaires de Lyon.

Gass, William H. (1970) "Philosophy and the Form of Fiction" in *Fiction and the Figures of Life*, New York, Alfred A. Knopf, 3–26.

Genette, Gérard (1969) *Figures* II, Paris, Seuil.

Genette, Gérard (1980) *Narrative Discourse: An Essay in Method*, Jane E. Lewin (trans.), Ithaca, Cornell University Press.

Genette, Gérard (1987) *Paratexts: Thresholds of Interpretation*, Jane E. Lewin (trans.), Cambridge, Cambridge University Press.

Genette, Gérard (1993) *Fiction and Diction*, Catherine Porter (trans.), Ithaca, Cornell University Press.

Genette, Gérard (1997) *Palimpsests: Literature in the Second Degree*, Channa Newman and Claude Doubinsky (trans.), Lincoln, University of Nebraska Press.

Genette, Gérard (2004) *Métalepses: De la figure à la fiction*, Paris, Seuil.

Goffman, Erving (1974), *Frame Analysis: An Essay on the Organization of Experience*, Cambridge, Harvard University Press.

Gratton, Johnnie (1986) "*Roland Barthes par Roland Barthes*: Autobiography and the Notion of Expression", *Romance Studies*, 4 (2): 57–65.

Gratton, Johnnie (2001) "Autofiction" in *Encyclopedia of Life Writing: Autobiographical and Biographical Forms*, Margaretta Jolly (ed.), London, Fitzroy Dearborn, vol. 1: A-K, 86–87.

Greenblatt, Stephen (1987) "Towards a Poetics of Culture", *Southern Review*, 20 (1): 3–15.

Greenblatt, Stephen (1988) *Shakespearean Negotiations*, Berkeley, University of California Press.

Greenblatt, Stephen (2005) *Renaissance Self-Fashioning: From More to Shakespeare*, Chicago, University of Chicago Press.

Gronemann, Claudia (2019) "Autofiction" in *Handbook of Autobiography/Autofiction*, Martina Wagner-Egelhaaf (ed.), Boston, De Gruyter, Vol. 1: 241–246.

Guibert, Hervé (1993) *My Parents*, Liz Heron (trans.), London, Serpent's Tail.

Haffen, Aude (2020) "Review of Autofiction in English", *Biography* 43 (4): 813–818.

Heidenreich, Rosemarin Elfriede (2018) *Literary Impostors: Canadian Autofiction of the Early 20th Century*, Montreal, McGill-Queen's University Press.

Hejinian, Lyn (2000) *The Language of Inquiry*, Berkeley, University of California Press.

Hejinian, Lyn (2013) *My Life and My Life in the Nineties*, Middletown, CT, Wesleyan University Press.

Herman, David (2013) *Storytelling and the Sciences of the Mind*, Cambridge, MIT Press.

Heti, Sheila (2012) *How Should a Person Be?*, Toronto, House of Anansi.

Hoffman, Anne Golomb (1992) "The Womb of Culture: Fictions of Identity and Their Undoing in Yehoshua's *Mr. Mani*", *Prooftexts* 12: 245–263.

Holland, Mary (2013) *Succeeding Postmodernism: Language and Humanism in Contemporary American Literature*, New York, Bloomsbury.

Holland, Norman N. (2012) *"Don Quixote* and the Neuroscience of Metafiction" in *Cognitive Literary Studies: Current Themes and New Directions*, Isabel Jaén and Julien Jacques Simon (eds), Austin, University of Texas Press, 73–88.

Hughes, Evan (2014) "Karl Ove Knausgaard Became a Literary Sensation by Exposing His Every Secret", *The New Republic*, 7 April 2014, https://newrepublic.com/a rticle/117245/karl-ove-knausgaard-interview-literary-star-struggles-regret, accessed 20 November 2021.

Hutcheon, Linda (1980) *Narcissistic Narrative: The Metafictional Paradox*, Waterloo, Wilfrid Laurier University Press.

Hutcheon, Linda (1984) "Canadian Historiographic Metafiction", *Essays on Canadian Writing*, 30 (30): 228.

Hutcheon, Linda (1988) *The Poetics of Postmodernism: History, Theory, Fiction*, New York, Routledge.

Jakobson, Roman (1978) "Closing Statement: Linguistics and Poetics" in *Style in Language*, Thomas A. Sebeok (ed.), Cambridge, MIT Press, 350–377.

James, Marlon (2014) *A Brief History of Seven Killings*, New York, Riverhead Books.

Jameson, Fredric (1991) *Postmodernism or, The Cultural Logic of Late Capitalism*, Durham, Duke University Press.

Jameson, Fredric (2013) *The Antinomies of Realism*, New York, Verso.

Jenkins, Keith (2003a) *Re-Thinking History*, London, Routledge Classics.

Jenkins, Keith (2003b) *Refiguring History: New Thoughts on an Old Discipline*, London, Routledge.

Johnson, Mat (2012) *Pym*, New York, Spiegel & Grau.

Jones, E. H. (2009) "Autofiction: A Brief History of a Neologism" in *Life Writing: Essays on Autobiography, Biography and Literature*, Richard Bradford (ed.), Basingstoke, Palgrave Macmillan, 174–184.

Jordan, Shirley (2012) "Etat Présent: Autofiction in the Feminine", *French Studies*, LXVII (1): 76–84.

Jouet, Jacques (2001) *Subway Poems*, Ian Monk (trans.), *SubStance*, 30 (3): 64–70.

Kacandes, Irene (2012) "Experimental Life Writing" in *The Routledge Companion to Experimental Literature*, Joe Bray, Alison Gibbons, and Brian McHale (eds), New York, Routledge, 380–392.

Keen, Suzanne (2007) *Empathy and the Novel*, New York, Oxford University Press.

Kellaway, Kate (2014) *"Interview"* with Rachel Cusk, www.theguardian.com/books/2014/a ug/24/rachel-cusk-interview-aftermath-outline, accessed 15 November 2021.

Knausgaard, Karl Ove (2014) *My Struggle*, Book 2, Don Bartlett (trans.), London, Vintage.

Knausgaard, Karl Ove (2018) *My Struggle*, Book 6, Don Bartlett and Martin Aitken (trans.), New York, Archipelago.

Lacan, Jacques (1977) *Écrits: A Selection*, Alan Sheridan (trans.), New York, W. W. Norton.

Laubender, Carolyn (2020) "Speak for Yourself: Psychoanalysis, Autotheory, and the Plural Self", *Arizona Quarterly*, 76 (1): 39–64.

Lecarme, Jacques (1993) "L'autofiction, un mauvais genre?" in *Autofiction & Cie*, Philippe Lejeune (ed.), Paris, RITM.

Lecarme, Jacques and Éliane Lecarme-Tabone (1999) *L'autobiographie*, Paris, Armand Colin.

Lehman, David (2005) "Anna K." in *When a Woman Loves a Man*, New York, Scribner, 42.

Lejeune, Philippe (1987) *Moi aussi*, Paris, Seuil.

Lejeune, Philippe (1989) *On Autobiography*, Katherine Leary (trans.), Minneapolis, University of Minnesota Press.

Lerner, Ben (2013) *Leaving the Atocha Station*, New York, Granta.

Lévesque-Jalbert, Emile (2020) "'This is not an autofiction': Autoteoría, French Feminism, and Living in Theory", *Arizona Quarterly*, 76 (1): 65–84.

Levy, Deborah (2013) *Things I Don't Want to Know*, London, Hamish Hamilton.

Levy, Deborah (2018) *The Cost of Living*, London, Hamish Hamilton.

Levy, Deborah (2019) *The Man Who Saw Everything*, London, Hamish Hamilton.

Levy, Deborah (2021a) *Real Estate*, London, Hamish Hamilton.

Levy, Deborah and Tash Aw (2021b) "*Deborah Levy on Real Estate*", https://www.youtube.com/watch?v=vq7o72vJY7Q, accessed 7 December 2021.

Lewis, Cara L. (2019) "Beholding: Visuality and Postcritical Reading in Ali Smith's *How to Be Both*", *Journal of Modern Literature*, 42 (3): 129–150.

Löschnigg, Martin (2010) "Postclassical Narratology and the Theory of Autobiography" in *Postclassical Narratology: Approaches and Analyses*, Jan Alber and Monika Fludernik (eds), Columbus, Ohio State University Press, 255–274.

Lukács, Georg (1962) *The Historical Novel*, Hannah and Stanley Mitchell (trans.), London, Merlin.

Lyotard, Jean-François (1984) *The Postmodern Condition: A Report on Knowledge*, Geoff Bennington and Brian Massumi (trans.), Minneapolis, University of Minnesota Press.

Machado, Carmen Maria (2019) *In the Dream House*, Minneapolis, Graywolf Press.

Marcoux, Jean-Philippe (2010) "Theoretical Constraint, Linguistic Copiousness: Reconsidering Section 'A' in Christian Bök's *Eunoia*", *Canadian Poetry*, 66: 87–97.

Marcus, Sharon & Stephen Best (2009) "Surface Reading: An Introduction", *Representations*, 108 (1): 1–21.

Martens, Lorna (2018) "Autofiction in the Third Person, with a Reading of Christine Brooke-Rose's *Remake*" in *Autofiction in English*, Hywel Dix (ed.), Poole, UK, Palgrave, 49–64.

McBride, James (2013) *The Good Lord Bird*, New York, Riverhead Books.

McCullough, Jet (2021) "A Gloomy Confidence: The Dual Treatment of Limits and [De]limiting in Lydia Davis's *Break It Down*", unpublished essay.

McEwan, Ian (2002) *Atonement*, New York, Vintage.

McHale, Brian (1987) *Postmodernist Fiction*, New York, Methuen.

McLaughlin, Robert L. (2012) "Post-Postmodernism" in *The Routledge Companion to Experimental Literature*, Joe Bray, Alison Gibbons, and Brian McHale (eds), New York, Routledge, 212–223.

Moi, Toril (2017a) *Revolution of the Ordinary: Literary Studies after Wittgenstein, Austin, and Cavell*, Chicago, University of Chicago Press.

Moi, Toril (2017b) "Describing *My Struggle*", *The Point*, 27 December 2017, https://thepointmag.com/criticism/describing-my-struggle-knausgaard/, accessed 20 November 2021.

Monk, Ian and Daniel Levin Becker, eds. (2018) *All That Is Evident Is Suspect: Readings from the Oulipo 1963–2018*, San Francisco, McSweeney's.

Morrison, Toni (1992) *Playing in the Dark: Whiteness and the Literary Imagination*, New York, Vintage.

Motte, Warren (1986) "Introduction" in *Oulipo: A Primer of Potential Literature* (trans. and ed.), London, Dalkey Archive Press, 1–22.

Motte, Warren (2009a) "Constraint on the Move", *Poetics Today*, 30 (4): 719–735.

Motte, Warren (2009b) "Playing in Earnest", *New Literary History*, 40 (1): 25–42.

Naughton, Gerald David (2018) "Posthistorical Fiction and Postracial Passing in James McBride's *The Good Lord Bird*", *Critique*, 59 (3): 346–354.

Neumann, Birgit and Ansgar Nünning (2012) "Metanarration and Metafiction" in *The Living Handbook of Narratology*, www.lhn.uni-hamburg.de/node/50.html, accessed 13 December 2021.

Nicol, Bran (2018) "Eye to I: American AF and Its Contexts from Jerzy Kosinski to Dave Eggers" in *Autofiction in English*, Hywel Dix (ed.), Poole, UK, Palgrave, 255–274.

Offill, Jenny (2014) *Dept. of Speculation*, New York, Knopf.

Paley, Grace (1994) "A Conversation with My Father" in *The Collected Stories*, New York, Farrar, Strauss and Giroux, 232–237.

Pamuk, Orhan (2001) *My Name Is Red*, Erdag Goknar (trans.), New York, Vintage Books.

Perec, Georges (1991) *Les Revenentes*, Paris, Julliard.

Perec, Georges (1994) *A Void*, Gilbert Adair (trans.), Boston, Verba Mundi.

Perec, Georges (2008) *La Disparition*, Paris, Gallimard.

Perelman, Bob (1993) "Parataxis and Narrative: The New Sentence in Theory and Practice", *American Literature*, 65 (2): 313–324.

Perelman, Bob (1996) *The Marginalization of Poetry*, Princeton, Princeton University Press.

Perloff, Marjorie (1991) *Radical Artifice: Writing Poetry in the Age of Media*, Chicago, University of Chicago Press.

Perloff, Marjorie (2004) "The Oulipo Factor: The Procedural Poetics of Christian Bök and Caroline Bergvall", *Textual Practice*, 18 (1): 23–45.

Pier, John (2016a) "Metalepsis" in *The Living Handbook of Narratology*, www.lhn.uni-hamburg.de/node/51.html, accessed 13 December 2021.

Pier, John (2016b) "Narrative Levels" in *The Living Handbook of Narratology*, www.lhn.uni-hamburg.de/node/32.html, accessed 13 December 2021.

Poe, Edgar Allan (2010) *The Narrative of Arthur Gordon Pym of Nantucket*, Peterborough, ON, Broadview Editions.

Puig, Manuel (1978) *Kiss of the Spider Woman*, Thomas Colchie (trans.), New York, Vintage.

Queneau, Raymond (1961) *Cent mille milliards de poèmes*, Paris, Gallimard.

Queneau, Raymond (1981) *Exercises in Style*, Barbara Wright (trans.), New York, New Directions.

Richardson, Brian (2015) *Unnatural Narrative: Theory, History, and Practice*, Columbus, Ohio State University Press.

Ricoeur, Paul (1970) *Freud and Philosophy: An Essay on Interpretation*, New Haven, Yale University Press.

Roffman, Karin (2017) *The Songs We Know Best: John Ashbery's Early Life*, New York, Farrar, Straus and Giroux.

Rothman, Joshua (2018) "Karl Ove Knausgaard Looks Back on 'My Struggle'", *The New Yorker*, 11 November, www.newyorker.com/culture/the-new-yorker-interview/karl-ove-knausgaard-the-duty-of-literature-is-to-fight-fiction, accessed 12 December 2021.

Ryan, Donal (2014) *The Spinning Heart*, Hanover, NH, Steerforth Press.

Ryan, Marie-Laure (2006) *Avatars of Story*, Minneapolis, University of Minnesota Press.

Sainsbury, Daisy (2017) "Constraints, Concealment, and Buried Texts: Reading Walter Abish with Georges Perec and the Oulipo", *Comparative Literature*, 69 (3): 303–314.

Saussure, Ferdinand de (1959) *Course in General Linguistics*, New York, McGraw-Hill.

Scholes, Robert, (1970) "Metafiction", *The Iowa Review*, 1 (4): 100–115.

Scholes, Robert (1979) *Fabulation and Metafiction*, Urbana, University of Illinois Press.

Sebald, W. G. (1997) *The Emigrants*, Michael Hulse (trans.), New York, New Directions.

Sebald, W. G. (2011) *Austerlitz*, Anthea Bell (trans.), New York, Modern Library.

Sedgwick, Eve Kosofsky (2003) *Touching Feeling: Affect, Pedagogy, Performativity*, Durham, Duke University Press.

Sidney, Philip (2000) *The Defense of Poesy* in *The Norton Anthology of English Literature*, 7th edition, vol. 1, M. H. Abrams and Stephen Greenblatt (eds), New York, Norton, 933–954.

Silliman, Ron (1977) *The New Sentence*, New York, Roof Books.

Silliman, Ron (2002) *Tjanting*, Great Barrington, MA, Figures.

Silliman, Ron (2008) *The Alphabet*, Tuscaloosa, University of Alabama Press.

Silver, Lucas (2021) "'Hungry Icons': Starving Girls, Hunger Artists, and Open-Ended Symbolism in 'Iconography' and 'A Hunger Artist'", unpublished essay.

Smith, Ali (2014) *How to Be Both*, New York, Anchor Books.

Smith, Sidonie and Julia Watson (2010) *Reading Autobiography: A Guide for Interpreting Life Narratives*, 2nd edition, Minneapolis, University of Minnesota Press.

Sommer, Roy (2020) "The (Un)natural Response: Reading Walter Abish's *Alphabetical Africa*" in *Unnatural Narratology: Extensions, Revisions, and Challenges*, Jan Alber and Brian Richardson (eds), Columbus, Ohio State University, 95–109.

Sontag, Susan (1982) "Against Interpretation" in *A Susan Sontag Reader*, New York, Vintage, 95–104.

Sturgeon, Jonathan (2014) "The Death of the Postmodern Novel and the Rise of Autofiction", *Flavorwire*, 31 December, http://flavorwire.com/496570/2014-the-death-of-the-postmodern-novel-and-the-rise-of-autofiction, accessed 1 November 2021.

Sturrock, John (1993) *Structuralism*, New York, Fontana Press.

Tate, James (2004) "The Rally" in *Return to the City of White Donkeys*, New York, Ecco, 88–89.

Tomkiw, Lydia (1988) "Six of Ox Is" in *The Best American Poetry*, John Ashbery (ed.), New York, Collier Books, 186.

Vincent, John Emil (2007) *John Ashbery and You: His Later Books*, Athens, University of Georgia Press.

Waldman, Katy (2019) "Carmen Maria Machado's Many Haunted Stories of a Toxic Relationship," *The New Yorker*, 31 October, www.newyorker.com/books/page-tur ner/carmen-maria-machados-many-haunted-stories-of-a-toxic-relationship, acces sed 21 November 2021.

Wallace, David Foster (1993) "A Conversation with David Foster Wallace by Larry McCaffery", *The Review of Contemporary Fiction*, 13 (2): 127–150.

Walonen, Michael K. (2018) "Violence, Diasporic Transnationalism, and Neo-Imperialism in *A Brief History of Seven Killings*", *Small Axe*, 22 (3): 1–12.

Waugh, Patricia (1984) *Metafiction: The Theory and Practice of Self-Conscious Fiction*, New York, Routledge.

Wheeler, Sara (1999) *Terra Incognita: Travels in Antarctica*, New York, Modern Library.

White, Hayden (1973) *Metahistory: The Historical Imagination in Nineteenth-Century Europe*, Baltimore, Johns Hopkins University Press.

White, Hayden (1978) "The Historical Text as Literary Artifact" in *Tropics of Discourse: Essays in Cultural Criticism*, Baltimore, Johns Hopkins University Press, 81–100.

Wiegman, Robyn (2020) "Introduction: Autotheory Theory", *Arizona Quarterly*, 76 (1): 1–14.

Wilks, Jennifer M. (2016) "'Black Matters': Race and Literary History in Mat John-son's *Pym*", *European Journal of American Studies*, 11 (1): 1–20.

Wimsatt, W. K. and M. C. Beardsley (1946) "The Intentional Fallacy", *The Sewanee Review*, 54 (3): 468–488.

Wolf, Werner (2009) "Metareference across Media" in *Metareference across Media: Theory and Case Studies*, Werner Wolf, Katharina Bantleon, and Jeff Thoss (eds), Amsterdam, Rodopi.

Wolf, Werner (2011) "Is There a Metareferential Turn, and, If So, How Can It Be Explained?" in *The Metareferential Turn in Contemporary Arts and Media: Forms, Functions, Attempts at Explanation*, Werner Wolf (ed.), Amsterdam, Rodopi, 1–47.

Woolf, Virginia (1942) "Professions for Women" in *The Death of the Moth and Other Essays*, London, Hogarth Press, 149–154.

Worthington, Marjorie (2017) "Fiction in the 'Post-Truth' Era: The Ironic Effects of Autofiction", *Critique*, 58 (5): 471–483.

Worthington, Marjorie (2018) *The Story of Me: Contemporary American Autofiction*, Lincoln, University of Nebraska Press.

Yehoshua, A. B. (1992) *Mr. Mani*, Hillel Halkin (trans.), New York, Harvest Book.

Yehoshua, A. B. (2001) "*Mr. Mani* and the Akedah", *Judaism: A Quarterly Journal*, 50 (1): 1–4.

Yu, Charles (2010) *How to Live Safely in a Science Fictional Universe*, New York, Vintage.

Zunshine, Lisa (2006) *Why We Read Fiction*, Columbus, Ohio State University Press.

INDEX

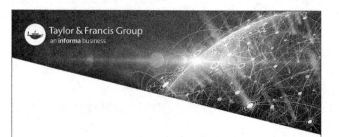

Printed in the United States
by Baker & Taylor Publisher Services